CLASSIC FABRICS

CLASSIC FABRICS

HENRIETTA SPENCER-CHURCHILL

To Karen

With Best Wishes
from

Henrietta Spencer-Churchill

November 1996.

RIZZOLI
NEW YORK

First published in the United States of America in 1996 by
Rizzoli International Publications, Inc.
300 Park Avenue South, New York, NY10010

First published in Great Britain in 1996 by
Collins & Brown Limited, London

1 3 5 7 9 8 6 4 2

Library of Congress Cataloging-in-Publication Data

Spencer-Churchill, Henrietta, 1958-
Classic Fabrics/Lady Henrietta Spencer-Churchill; photographs by Andreas von Einsiedel.
p. cm.
Includes bibliographical references.
ISBN 0-8478-1974-4 (HC)
1. Textile fabrics—History.   2. Textile fabrics in interior decoration   I.
Title
NK8806.S64 1996
746—dc20   96-18122
                                                CIP

Project editor Alexandra Parsons
Designer Christine Wood
Special photography Andreas von Einsiedel
Stylist Jacky Boase
Picture researcher Philippa Lewis

Reproduction by Daylight Colour, Singapore
Printed and bound in the United Kingdom by Jarrolds

CONTENTS

Introduction 6

FABRICS IN HISTORY 11
Early Fabrics 12
17th Century 14
18th Century 18
19th Century 24
A Design Revolution 30

FABRICS IN THE HOME 35
Living Rooms 37
Studies and Dens 62
Dining Rooms 66
Halls and Landings 76
Bedrooms 80
Bathrooms 100
Gardens 106

THE FABRICS 113
Tapestry 114
Embroidery 118
Quilting and Patchwork 122
Laces and Voiles 125
Velvet 128
Damasks and Brocades 132
Silk 138
Patterned Weaves 144
Wool 150
Printed Cotton and Chintz 156
Linens 166
Checks 172
Stripes 174
Paisleys 176
Trimmings 178

Glossary 184
Acknowledgements 188
Index 189

Introduction

It is difficult to imagine a room without a scrap of fabric – no drapes, no soft surfaces, no subtle textures or patterns and, above all, none of the powerful associations that we make between fabrics and atmosphere. Thick brocades and handwoven tapestries evoke a sense of past grandeur; velvets and chenilles feel luxuriously warm; tartan rugs are cosy and comforting, lace and flower-sprigged cottons have a spring-like freshness. When choosing fabrics for the home, I think these associations should be put to work, and in my view, the type and texture of the fabric is just as important as the colour and pattern.

THE HISTORICAL PERSPECTIVE

It is interesting that the development of furnishing textiles relates closely to historical changes in the social and economic climate. The earliest textiles were produced for practical purposes – for clothing and shelter – and the cloths produced in early times were products of the natural resources and skills available in particular regions. As skills and technology developed, so did the quality and design of textiles, and as trade grew, so did outside influences on merchants and artisans alike. Silks, for instance, originated in the Chinese province of Shantung; flax grew in the silt of the Nile delta; cotton blossomed in India; while the production of wool was a speciality of English and northern European weavers.

As trade between countries increased, so did competition and imitation. Fabric designs tended to follow those in architecture, from the dramatic Gothic via the Rococo swirls of damask to the simple Palladian elegance of Georgian times. Then came a nineteenth-century passion for all things exotic, and the overworked fuss of the Victorians followed by a clean break with the past and the formation of the Arts and Crafts and *Art Nouveau* movements.

FABRICS IN THE HOME

Today, of course, we can have our pick of everything. Man-made yarns with amazing hardwearing properties can be unobtrusively mixed with the finest silks and linens, blending to create expensive fabrics practical for everyday use. The market for

reproductions of historic fabrics has given us a comprehensive range of new material based on archive designs to enhance any period interior. Modern printing and dyeing technology has led to patterns in endless colourways, and a choice between crisp clear outlines or a softly faded, lived-in pattern perfectly at home in the classic English country house. For the individualist, talented craftspeople can produce hand-dyed, hand-printed, specially woven cloths of great originality, and beautiful hand-knotted fringes and tassels to match any scheme.

CLASSIC FABRICS

With this book, I hope to demonstrate the endless possibilities that present themselves when creating a look with fabrics. There are ideas on recreating period interiors, putting together monochrome schemes with splashes of colour, mixing the old with the new and patterns with patterns. Rooms covered entirely in tartans and others in Toile de Jouy, pale and pretty bedrooms, elegant drawing rooms, warm, welcoming dens and smart masculine retreats are featured. Some rooms cost very little to put together, with an abundance of cheap fabrics such as calico and muslin, and some rooms are full of costly brocades, beautiful tapestries and swathes of shimmering silks. Awkwardly-sized rooms are made to look perfectly elegant thanks to imaginative window treatments, and rooms of beautiful proportions are enhanced with the simplest of drapes. The choice of fabric is always the starting point for the decorative schemes seen in these pages.

The book also includes practical advice on the choice of fabrics for the classic interior, and their suitability for various household applications from curtaining and upholstery to throws, bedcovers and table cloths. I hope that in this book you will find information and inspiration in equal measure.

Fabrics in History

The story of household textiles starts with the simple human need to be warm and comfortable. Once that need had been met, fabrics became an art form and then, inevitably, a status symbol. Advances in technology ensured an explosion in demand for every type of fabric in every possible taste and style. Looking back at the origins of classic fabrics, helps us to set them in context today.

EARLY FABRICS

ABOVE *This detail from a 16th-century cushion cover at Hardwick Hall, illustrates part of* The Sacrifice of Isaac. *The embroidery is typical of the period, depicting a beautifully detailed Biblical scene, worked in subtle, natural dye colours.*

COMPARATIVELY FEW SAMPLES of Medieval textiles have withstood the ravages of damp, sunlight and time. The fragments that have survived tend to be the most precious – rich ceremonial fabrics belonging to church and royalty. Visual evidence in contemporary art, and descriptions of household fabrics in wills and inventories, help us to build up a picture of how they were used. From these sources it is evident that even the noblest homes were sparsely furnished and fairly uncomfortable. Fabrics were used mainly for wall hangings, bed coverings and bed curtains.

It is harder to recreate a picture of less elevated interiors, but we can be sure that there too wall hangings and bed coverings were a practical necessity. In castle and cottage, wall hangings provided much-needed warmth and draught-proofing. Modest homes had hangings of coarse linen woven from flax, left natural or dyed a single colour. More opulent households boasted magnificent tapestries and luxurious hangings of silk and velvet.

WOOLLEN TAPESTRIES

The most desirable wall hangings were woollen tapestries, and we know that these were made in France from the 14th century onwards, remaining essential items of furnishing until the 18th century. Much art and invention went into the designs of tapestries, the grandest of which incorporated real gold thread. The Medieval love of

the natural world was reflected in the exquisite delineation of animals and flowers. Scenes of courtly life were popular, often depicting knights and their ladies setting forth into an idealised landscape for hunting or romantic dalliance. Biblical scenes were often chosen for churches and private chapels, and scenes from ancient history were thought to convey a degree of learning.

EMBROIDERIES

The richest embroideries were worked on silks, satins and velvet. Some embroidery was done in noble households and convents, but there were also workshops in many towns dedicated to the craft. More fragile and ephemeral than woollen tapestries, the glorious richness of much of this work can only be guessed at through contemporary descriptions. A manuscript dating from 1416 describes the Duc de Berry's sumptuous red satin bed hangings, fantastically embroidered with bears and lions moving through tall pine trees. On a less extravagant scale, much embroidery was worked with coloured wools on linen, the most famous of which is the confusingly named Bayeux Tapestry – in fact an embroidery worked in chain, stem and split stitches. Towards the end of the 16th century, embroidered cloths were also used for covering chair cushions and pillows, and for throwing over tables – these early table cloths were known as table carpets.

SUPPLY AND DEMAND

The 15th century saw the end of the feudal system and the rise of a middle class in England. Wealthy merchants and farmers now wished to make their homes a testament to their status. Although the finest textiles were still imported, increased demand led to the establishment of a home-grown industry. The once-powerful textile guilds could no longer keep a tight grip on the industry. Ambitious entrepreneurs set up in business, supplying local craftsmen and women with the raw materials to spin and weave, passing the woven cloth on to other specialists for dyeing, printing or embroidering. Trade with other countries increased with inevitable cross-fertilisation of designs and techniques. By the end of the 16th century, the European textile industry was dynamic and flourishing, and Italy, the epicentre of the Renaissance, was at the forefront in matters of design and style.

BELOW *Two late 16th-century velvet appliqué roundels, the centres depicting birds and foliage. These details form part of a large panel at Hardwick Hall.*

FAR LEFT *A late 15th-century illumination to* Froissart's Chronicle of England and France, *depicting Richard II yielding the crown to the Earl of Derby. The two wall hangings in the background, most probably woollen tapestries, show just how colourful medieval interiors were.*

LEFT *This beautiful Tudor embroidery was originally a cushion cover. The background is velvet and the appliqué work is silk.*

13

17TH CENTURY

A GENERAL RISE IN THE STANDARD of living encouraged the continuing development of the textile trade in Europe. England dominated the woollen industry, Italy became the principal producer of silk and France, under Louis XIV, dominated the luxury textile market. The French now became arbiters of taste and the rest of Europe followed their lead. In Britain, Huguenot and Flemish weavers, refugees from the French religious wars, brought with them not only French style, but also new techniques, such as the art of silk weaving. New ideas for the decoration of interiors were often engraved on copper plates and sold as sets of prints, disseminating ideas in the way magazines do today.

A sense of unified design emerged during this period. Wall decoration, furnishings and architectural features were beginning to be considered together as a piece. A description of Madame de Rambouillet's *chambre bleu* in her Paris house, finished in the 1620s, tells of wall-hangings of blue velvet patterned in gold with matching table carpet and upholstered chairs.

WINDOWS AND WALLS

Classically-inspired architecture changed the proportions of rooms – windows became increasingly important and numerous as a result of developments in the manufacture of larger panes of flat, clear glass. In the early part of the century, shutters alone blocked out light and cold, but towards the end of the century curtains were becoming commonplace. Starting as simple drapes – a single curtain attached to a rod by loops or rings sewn onto the fabric – pairs of curtains soon followed, and as time went by these became elaborately fringed and tasselled. The festoon curtain was a French idea, usually teamed with an elaborate wooden or fabric pelmet to conceal the workings at the top.

Hangings, typically of damask, velvet, tapestry or worsted, remained an important element in interior decoration, but gradually other options were deemed fashionable. Walls of this period might be decorated with plasterwood, *boiserie* (wood panelling), lacquer or paint effects such as marbling.

UPHOLSTERY

The upholsterer was the craftsman responsible for all work involving fabric. He undertook not only the fixing of wall hangings but also the upholstery of chairs and beds. The bed remained the most prestigious piece of furniture in the house. The grandest households boasted a bedchamber used exclusively as a reception room, where the richest fabrics and trimmings reflected glory on the owner.

Furniture was now typically upholstered in matching sets. The chairs of the period, the so-called 'farthingale' chairs, had a properly upholstered seat and back rest. Furniture was still sparse, and when not in use, the chairs would be ranged against the walls – there is a tell-tale lack of finish to such chairs when viewed from

ABOVE *Queen Anne's bedroom at Dyrham Park. The bedhangings are the original rich crimson and yellow velvet dating from 1710.*

RIGHT *The State bed of James II, made in 1673, with its original bedhangings of silk tissue or* lampas *embroidered with silver .*

BELOW *This Dutch interior painted c. 1630 shows a bedchamber in a rich merchant's house made comfortable with woven tapestry furnishings and bed hangings.*

ABOVE *These beautiful carved walnut chairs from Knole are enhanced by rich silk damask fabric and tassel fringing. The fabric is now so worn it is difficult to identify the large Baroque design.*

behind. Caned chairs and daybeds, which became fashionable towards the end of the century, were given squab cushions for greater comfort, typically covered with woollen velvet, moquette or turkeywork.

Fabrics at this time were manufactured in narrow widths. For this reason braids and fringing became vastly popular as they disguised the frequent seams and joins in the upholsterer's work neatly and decoratively. Trimmings ranged from plain woven wool and silk braids to elaborate gold and silver lace.

RIGHT *Part of the Diogenes Room at Dyrham Park, a National Trust property in Avon. The fine pair of William III walnut chairs that flank the Delft pyramid flower vases, are covered in their original crimson Genoese silk velvet and trimmed with a gold fringe. The magnificent tapestry after which the room is named, shows Diogenes meeting Alexander the Great. It is an English work, woven at Mortlake.*

BELOW *The Queen's Closet at Ham House. This is part of a suite of rooms built on and decorated for a proposed visit by Catherine of Braganza in 1675. The walls are hung with the original fabric, a French Jacquard weave red silk damask with silver thread embroidery and silver fringing.*

18TH CENTURY

THE EARLY 18TH CENTURY saw continued growth in the textile industry as the quality and variety of designs improved, largely due to an ever-increasing demand for comfort in the home. Luxurious furnishings were produced throughout Europe to meet this growing market. In France, exquisite woven silks were manufactured at Lyon, carpets were woven at Savonnerie and tapestries were worked at Gobelins and Beauvais. From Genoa in Italy came the finest damasks and velvets, while England dominated the market for woollen goods.

As the century progressed, continental Europe embraced the Rococo style, with its flamboyant curlicues and scrollwork. Britain and America, however, followed the classical style, which developed into the look loosely termed 'Georgian'.

BELOW *The First State Room at Blenheim Palace, showing one of a series of tapestries celebrating the First Duke of Marlborough's military campaigns. They were woven in Brussels. The gilt furniture is French, and covered in both tapestry and Utrecht velvet with the Sun King motif. The carpet is a French Savonnerie.*

LEFT *This beautifully carved gilt sofa was designed by Robert Adam for the State Drawing Room at Kedleston Hall in Derbyshire. The stunning blue silk damask is a copy of the original fabric.*

BELOW *The Antechamber, or Tapestry Room, at Osterley Park, Middlesex, where Gobelins tapestries designed by the great French Rococo painter, François Boucher, are displayed. The medallions on the wall show the dawn goddess Aurora discovering the hunter Cephalus and Pomona, goddess of gardens, being wooed by Vertumnus, the god of Spring. The tapestries on the chairs were woven for Madame de Pompadour.*

INFORMAL COMFORT

This period was defined by the decreasing formality in the way people entertained. Forbiddingly impressive grand State Rooms were now to be found only in royal palaces, not in the homes of nobles or the landed gentry. Rooms were now required where people could enjoy themselves: space was needed for dancing, card-playing, private conversations, informal meals and privacy from the eyes of servants. This relaxed attitude offered a wider range of opportunities for interior decoration. One immediate bonus was the appearance of comfortable chairs and sofas to sink into, with smooth, round, upholstered arms, backs and seats.

As the only source of heat was an open fire, the damage caused by soot and ash to expensive upholstery must have been considerable. A practical answer to this problem was adopted, and protective loose covers of checked or striped linen became popular for everyday use. Lighter colours and simpler fabrics were also used for a seasonal change of summer loose covers.

LEFT *The State Bedchamber at Nostell Priory was designed and decorated by the famous cabinetmaker Thomas Chippendale. He made the green lacquer furniture and designed the magnificent Rococo mirror. The printed silk bedhangings are similar in style to the originals.*

BELOW *The Blue Drawing Room at Woburn Abbey, was restored to its original 18th-century glory in the 1950s. The fabrics are faithful reproductions of the originals.*

ABOVE *This painting by Jean-François de Troy, dated 1752, shows a lady in her boudoir entertaining her suitor. Gorgeous velvets, gauzy lace and embroidered damasks add a glorious richness to an elegant 18th-century interior.*

WALL COVERINGS

Tapestries remained popular in the grandest interiors, although designs now reflected a much lighter spirit. Uplifting allegories and dour battle scenes gave way to depictions of *fêtes champêtres* and the four seasons. Tapestry was also being designed in smaller pieces for use as chair or cushion covers. Walls were still hung with fabrics, but changed seasonally – velvets for winter and taffetas for summer. In the mid-18th century, paper wall coverings became the height of fashion. Early designs merely mimicked textile patterns. English flock wallpapers with damask patterns were popular, as were hand-painted Chinese papers that imitated needlework. Eventually wallpapers were manufactured to match printed cotton and chintz upholstery fabrics.

DRAPERY

Bed hangings were still the focus of much attention, but instead of the stiff, almost sculpted look of the past, upholsterers were mastering the art of drapery. Free-standing four-poster beds gave way to beds placed against the wall, often in a niche, so that elaborate draperies could be supported by a canopy attached to the wall, and held in place by beautiful corded rosettes and tassels.

The fashion for complex draperies spread to curtains which became increasingly light and gauzy. Wall niches were often decorated with purely ornamental drapes. Elaborate tassels appeared on the cord pulls of window blinds, which were now being used to protect fabrics from the bleaching effect of sunlight streaming through ever-larger window openings.

ABOVE *This light and airy bedroom is in Mount Vernon, Virginia, the lovely home of George Washington, America's first president. The room is typical of the classical restraint of late 18th-century American interiors. By this time, lighter, flowing fabrics were being used for bedhangings and curtains.*

RIGHT *Princess Sophia Albertina's bedroom at Gripsholm Castle outside Stockholm. It was decorated in 1782 with these curtains and wall coverings of costly hand-painted Chinese silk. The portrait is a Gobelins tapestry depicting Louis XV.*

Towards the end of the 18th century, taste in Europe and America came together to a certain extent in an enthusiasm for Neo-Classicism, typified by the style of Robert Adam, which took its inspiration from Greek and Roman architecture and the discovery of Roman sites such as Pompeii and Herculaneum, all of which resulted in a cooler, more elegant interior style.

ABOVE *Unlined cotton voile curtains trimmed with a bobble fringe are typical of the period. This Scandinavian interior has hand-painted walls complemented by the striped fabric on the bench seats.*

19TH CENTURY

WHEN VIEWED AS A WHOLE, the 19th century runs the most astonishing gamut of styles, starting with confident Regency elegance, and followed by a revivalist frenzy for the Medieval, Gothic and Rococo, allied to a passion for all things oriental. It was an age of discovery and huge enthusiasms, most of which were reflected in some way in domestic interiors.

During the early part of the century, the French retained their position as the arbiters of taste for Europe. The fashion for drapery continued in ever-more elaborate schemes, even extending to the bedecking of ceilings, tent style. Long french windows were dressed with light muslin or voile inner curtains, surmounted by elaborate draped arrangements which remained fixed. These stiff, heavy, outer curtains were fashionably of two contrasting colours, the 'lining' being revealed in the complex swagging. It was common for a wall with two windows to be treated with a continuous line of drapery, joining the windows in one decorative sweep. Elaborate fringing, netting and tassels completed the overall look.

ABOVE *The two-colour silk curtains in this elegant room, trimmed with a matching two-colour fringe, are typical of the elaborate draperies of the period. The house, completely decorated in the 19th-century Biedermeier style, is part of the Skansen museum complex in Stockholm.*

RIGHT *Luxurious voile curtains and draped pelmets are ideal for this elegant interior as they do not detract from, nor fight with, the fine details of the delicate 'Etruscan' painted decorations.*

FAR RIGHT *This elegant tail drapery in rich plain blue silk taffeta is backed with a striking red fabric and trimmed with a bobble fringe. This treatment is ideal for framing an elegant window and turning it into a dramatic focal point. The single voile curtain draped to one side adds softness and, on a practical note, will help to filter harsh sunlight. The room is in Homewood House, Baltimore, built in 1801 as a wedding gift from a generous father to the original owner, Charles Carroll Jr.*

FAST-CHANGING FASHION

Leading architects and designers produced patterns for furniture and designs for interiors in every style, and these in turn influenced the manufacturers of fabrics and wallpapers. Floral designs continued to be popular, largely due to the influx of exotic flowers and plants brought back by intrepid 19th-century travellers to flourish in the hothouses and botanical gardens of Europe and America.

Thanks to new technology, there was an enormous variety of fabrics available, and at the same time so much was being written about 'good taste', that many people became totally confused. It became quite common to select a style to suit the nature of the room: thus the Greek Revival or Gothic style might be deemed suitably serious for a library, while Rococo was considered more engagingly frivolous for a lady's boudoir, and Medieval style was thought to conjure up the right atmosphere for dining.

BELOW *The rich blue custom-made silk fabric on the walls and chairs is woven with gold medallions. It provides a wonderful background for the gilt-framed paintings in this magnificent room at Het Loo, a royal palace in Holland. The strong blues and greens are typical of the 1820s and 30s.*

A MANUFACTURING BOOM

The mid-19th century was a time of consolidation in the textile industry. Machinery was developed to speed up manufacture, and printing and dyeing processes were also undergoing a technological revolution. The Great Exhibition, held in London in 1851, showed examples of machine-made fabrics from all over the world, in a vast variety of styles, quality and taste. The exhibit had mixed reviews, with many experts criticising the poor quality and ugly designs. In retrospect, it was an opportunity for manufacturers to show off the capabilities of their new-fangled machinery without too much consideration for design or colour sense.

LEFT *A watercolour of an interior by Lili Cartwright painted in 1845, shows a mid-19th-century drawing room furnished in a style typical of the period. It was commonplace at this time to mix different patterns and fabrics in one room.*

27

VICTORIAN STYLE

In the late 19th century, the characteristically over-ornamented, over-stuffed 'Victorian' taste held sway. Typical is the development of the easy chair, gently reclining and extremely comfortable, the upholstery a miracle of springs and deep buttoning. Ottomans, corner stools and love seats appeared in profusion. The style of upholstery required heavy, dark fabrics such as wool damask, merino and plush. Printed cottons were reserved for the bedroom and were unlikely to be found in downstairs reception rooms. Curtains became heavier and stiffer, the floating muslins and voiles being reduced to utilitarian nets. Pelmets, often made of stiffened fabric and cut into scrolls and scallops, were decorated with ornamental braid, and even the mantelpiece was treated to a velvet pelmet or a silk frill.

Embroidered bell-pulls, piano covers, footstools, table cloths and antimacassars were testament to the many hours spent by Victorian ladies at their crochet and embroidery frames with a mission to beautify their homes.

ABOVE *This dressing table in Her Ladyship's Room at Lanhydrock in Cornwall is a faithful copy of the Victorian original. It is covered in a lace fabric from a specialist lace-making firm in Scotland.*

RIGHT *The Saloon at Castle Ward in County Down, Ireland, is a wonderful example of Gothic Revival style. The chenille table covering is characteristic of the Victorian interior.*

BELOW *This room is in Victoria House, Portland, Maine. Deep plush buttoning was as popular in America at this time as it was in Britain and Europe.*

A DESIGN REVOLUTION

ABOVE *'Sweetness and light' – a comfortable and pretty design style perfectly captured in 'The Visit' by Sir George Clausen.*

ABOVE *Embroidery hanging worked in 1908 after 'The Mill', a painting by Sir Edward Burne-Jones. The rush-seated 'Sussex' chair was designed by Morris and Co.*

B Y THE 1870S THERE WAS A NEW aesthetic awareness in artistic circles, and the proliferation of over-ornamented machine-made goods began to be questioned. Influential critics condemned the poor quality of design and the sameness of mass production. The English art critic, John Ruskin, argued at considerable length that manufactured products lacked character and that accuracy in a design was unimportant. In Britain, a desire for simplicity emerged; in France, however, style continued to be influenced by the past until the emergence there of Art Nouveau.

THE ARTS AND CRAFTS MOVEMENT

A group of artists, designers and architects, among them the artist/craftsman William Morris, was inspired to design fabrics and wallpapers using traditional methods, natural materials and simple designs which concentrated on colour and texture. Motifs came from the Medieval period (Morris had a passion for Gothic cathedrals) and the natural world. This movement became generally known as the Arts and Crafts movement. Old dyeing techniques were revived using vegetable dyes, in a reaction against the crude and sometimes violent colourings of aniline dyes. Eschewing the shine and gloss of the manufactured finish, they introduced softly-coloured block-printed linens and double-woven wool cloths.

Designers such as Morris restored a dignity and quality to the decorative arts not seen since the finesse and style of the 18th century had been engulfed by an over-enthusiasm for industrialised processes. The problem with this attempt to put the brake on wholesale centralised manufacture, was that the work of Arts and Crafts groups was necessarily limited in quantity, but its influence was wide-reaching.

In America, a similar cry for greater simplicity had been made by Charles Eastlake in his book *Hints on Household Taste*, and groups such as the Roycrofters and Gustav Stickley's Craftsman Workshops had similar aspirations. The leading American designers at this time, Candace Wheeler, Louis Comfort Tiffany, Lockwood de Forest and Samuel Coleman, founded a company called Associated Artists which, like Morris's company in England, set out to employ skilled artists rather than industrial designers to create furnishings and fabrics for the home.

In both England and America there was a revival of embroidery or 'Art Needlework' as it was termed. Ladies' embroidery societies in Boston, New York and Philadelphia, and organisations such as the Royal School of Needlework in London, encouraged the making of exquisite, freely-designed pieces, using wonderful muted colours, for hangings, cushions and bedcovers.

ABOVE *A perfect example of the Arts and Crafts design philosophy. This room is in Standen, a house designed by Philip Webb, a close friend of William Morris. The silk curtains, embroidered to a Morris design hang on simple wooden poles. Arts and Crafts plates are displayed on the panelled chimney piece, and a fine example of art needlework screens the fire.*

STYLE FOR ALL

Much of the work of the Arts and Crafts movement is evident in the general style, often referred to as 'Queen Anne', that evolved on both sides of the Atlantic at the end of the century. This style claimed to embody all that was simple, artistic, appropriate and unfussy. 'Sweetness and light' were its guiding principles: woodwork and walls were painted white or light, simple plain coloured fabrics and pretty chintzes were featured, and window treatments were plain. Georgian-style furniture was admired and much was made of comfort and cosiness – upholstered window seats, inglenook fireplaces and cosy corners were all the rage. The style was so popular it was soon mass-produced and made available to all through the newly-established shopping phenomenon, the department store.

ART NOUVEAU

In Europe, the reaction against relying on the past for inspiration gave birth to *Art Nouveau*. The name of the movement was taken from a shop opened by Samuel Bing in Paris in 1895 called *La Maison de l'Art Nouveau*. His merchandise was designed by a group of artists and designers (among them Tiffany, famous for his lamps) who,

ABOVE AND RIGHT *Rooms from Hill House, designed and decorated by one of the leading and most influential architect/designers of the turn of the century, Charles Rennie Mackintosh. He was the leader of the 'Glasgow' school and his design influence spread from Scotland to Germany and Austria. Mackintosh left nothing to chance: he not only designed the house but everything inside it, from the architectural detailing of the cornices and window frames to the furniture, fittings and fabrics down to the lampshades and bedcovers.*

inspired by the liberating style of the Arts and Crafts movement, produced a stylised look influenced by Japanese designs and the sinuous asymmetric lines and curves of the Rococo period. It took Europe, particularly France and Belgium, by storm.

THE OLD AND THE NEW

In America and Britain the new direction in interiors was clear by the early years of the 20th century. Light clean lines and clearly defined areas of ornament – no more of the wild pattern-on-pattern excesses of the early Victorian age. It became positively fashionable not always to embrace the new, and to incorporate antiques as decorative pieces. English country houses reverted to the comfortable Georgian style, with printed cottons and chintzes now welcomed back into the living room. The introduction of electricity must also have been an influence, eliminating the fumes and smoke emanating from old gas and oil lamps. It also meant the fabric lampshade became a new decorative feature. In the new, cleaner house (for this is also the period of proprietary cleaners and labour-saving machines) most of the dark, heavy draperies disappeared for ever, particularly in the bedroom where bed curtains, for so long the pride of every household, were now considered old-fashioned and unhygenic.

BELOW *Simplicity, Shaker style. The beautifully-crafted furniture and the simple natural fabrics have their own enduring charm. Nothing in a Shaker house was unnecessary, or purely decorative.*

Fabrics in the Home

Fabrics are an instant style statement and the way in which they are hung or used as upholstery will make a luxurious difference to any home. Even inexpensive fabrics can transform a room if made up with imagination. Strong colours bring vibrancy and warmth, pale colours a calm sense of space. Every room in the house has its own style and atmosphere, and whatever the chosen ambiance, there is a fabric to set the right mood.

LIVING ROOMS

In rooms that are used every day by family and friends, a comfortable and welcoming atmosphere is vital. It is in a living room that the character of a home is established, so the textures and colours of fabrics need to be chosen with special care. Choose upholstery fabrics that are up to the task, and have them Scotchguarded if they are likely to be subject to heavy wear. Throws can add an extra dash of colour, and protect vulnerable areas such as arms and seat backs. Curtains will make an enormous impact, as living room windows tend to be large, so choose a fabric that is easy to live with and one that co-ordinates well with other colours and patterns.

LEFT *In this light and sunny country drawing room, a yellow silk has been chosen for the curtains and the elegant swags and tails of the pelmet. The curtains are trimmed with a three-colour cut fringe of crimson, yellow and green with a braided top. Yellow drag-finished walls and a white ceiling help to give the room added height. The sofa is covered in a traditional floral chintz, and all the other colours in the room are taken from this fabric. Armchairs are covered in a plain green strié linen with a bullion fringe set onto the straight skirt. The rugs were specially made to divide what is a long, narrow room into two distinct seating areas. The wide borders incorporate colours and floral motifs taken from the chintz.*

PREVIOUS PAGE *Pleated swags and tails are fixed onto the gilt poles and finials. As this room has low ceilings, it was important not to make the swags too deep, which would have blocked out both light and view. The depth of a pelmet should always be in proportion with the length of the curtains. Here a delicate balance has been struck between aesthetic and practical considerations.*

LEFT *The base of the tail has been lined with a contrasting fabric for emphasis. The lining is a striped moiré which is repeated on other furnishings in the room.*

RIGHT *The double tassel tiebacks match the three-colour fringing on the swags and tails. Buttoned horsehair seat cushions are covered in a check moiré from the same fabric range as the stripe moiré lining the curtain tails. The room may look as if all the different colours, patterns and fabric types have come together by happy accident, but every detail has been meticulously planned.*

BELOW *Continuing the check and stripe theme, the deep-buttoned round stool is covered in the check moiré. The stool is firmly upholstered, so with a tray on top, it can easily double as a coffee table.*

LEFT *A rich, gold-coloured plain silk was used for the curtains and pelmets in this welcoming, red and gold country drawing room. The two armchairs are covered in a floral chintz and the gathered skirts are trimmed top and bottom with a two-colour fan edge. The red sofa is upholstered in a heavier-weight linen mix fabric, and the fabric on the gold sofa is a jacquard weave. Both sofas have deep bullion fringing around their bases. The scatter cushions are made up from a selection of left-over fabrics and trimmings. and the carpet is an unobtrusively patterned Brussels weave.*

In this room there is a wonderful, rich mixture of plain gold silk, linen, cotton floral chintz and big bold stripes – and they all work brilliantly together. When choosing a variety of fabrics for a room, make up a swatch board with samples of the fabrics and paint colours to check that colours and patterns complement one another.

LEFT *Another view of the room shown on the previous page. These wonderfully extravagant dress curtains are made from the same luscious gold silk as the window curtains. The dramatic upward sweep of the pelmet gives extra height to the door and the central fan pleat sets off the whole scheme. The curtains are full, and the additional width makes the door look wider without obstructing the opening, so the doorway has become an impressive focal point. The swags are lined in a cream silk and the two colours are reflected in the subtle contrasting tones used for the paintwork. The bold stripes of the tablecloth, with its rich gold bullion fringe, add a dash of colour.*

In contrast is the pretty antique painted chair in the foreground, upholstered in a

delicately patterned velvet. Simple, white silk pleated lampshades add an understated yet classic touch, drawing attention to the white silk lining the curtains and the cornices and panelling which have been highlighted in a creamy white.

ABOVE *A detail of the pelmets over the windows. The cut fringe, made from a combination of silk and rayon, has a braided top. A matching rope trim forms a perfect edge to the pleated band from which the swags and tails are suspended. The fabric rosette, made by scrunching up the two colours of silk, makes a good textural contrast to the flat, pleated band at the top, and adds a welcome softness to the smart, squared-off corners.*

RIGHT *These rich, full, interlined curtains, linking a wall of matching windows, are in a Colefax and Fowler printed linen in soft, sunny shades of yellow and white. The pelmet is shaped to follow the line of the windows – longer where there is a wall between them, and shorter in front of the windows themselves – in order to let in the maximum amount of light and cut off the minimum amount of view. The pelmet is edged with a two-colour cut fringe, and the tiebacks, made by plaiting two softly padded lengths of the curtain fabric, are fixed low to relate to the window sills.*

ABOVE *A detail of the goblet-headed pelmet, with a simple rope stitched along the line of the headings for added emphasis. These goblets are small and the linking rope suits them perfectly. To draw attention to larger, deeper goblets, rope trims can be stitched in a knot on the front of each goblet – it can look very effective.*

LEFT *An elegant, gently bowed window with curtains, swags and tails in a stunning ivory damask, made from a hardwearing and practical mixture of cotton and viscose. The swags and tails are trimmed with a cotton bullion fringe and the curtains held back with a matching single tassel rope tieback. A splash of ice-blue moiré lining the tails picks up the blue in the striped damask used to upholster the sofa, a colour repeated in some of the scatter cushions.*

Pale tones predominate, giving the room a light, airy feeling, and maximising the shape and size of the magnificent window. The pale theme is carried though in every detail, from the white silk pleated lampshades to the white china pot-pourri dishes and the bouquet of white flowers.

The rug was custom-made from a standard colour Brussels weave trellis design, with an added border of scrolling pale blue leaves to finish the edges and define the seating area. The shiny old gold lacquer finish of the coffee table is the only area of strong colour in the room.

BELOW *Two elegant fauteuils stand in the bow window either side of the gilded table. They have been covered in a lovely tapestry fabric, the edging self-piped with a double row of piping. The cream-coloured background is a good contrast to the warm, natural wood finish, and the subtle greens and blues of the delicate floral design echo the colours used in the rest of the room.*

BELOW *The striped and stylised floral damask used for the sofa is in appropriately pale shades of cream and ice blue. These colours are given emphasis in the fabrics used to cover the scatter cushions. Self-piping defines the shape of the sofa and the cushions with subtlety. The deep cotton bullion fringe on the straight skirt of the sofa is a perfect colour match.*

TOP *The curtains in the room pictured on the previous page are held back with a single tassel two-tone tieback. Tiebacks are not just for practical purposes – they also give the curtains a distinct shape.*

RIGHT AND ABOVE *This serpentine arm Knole-style sofa is covered in a damask fabric with a blue strié background. A natural cotton single tassel tieback holds sides and back together, and a matching rope cord defines the shape of the seat cushions.*

LEFT *Three tall windows, with elaborate and perfectly proportioned swag and tail draperies, have become the focal point in this elegant London apartment drawing room. The windows could have been treated as one, but then the stack at each side would have been much bulkier, cutting out light. The fabric is a yellow silk taffeta which hangs beautifully, and reflects natural light from its shiny surface.*

RIGHT *The individual swags and tails were designed to work well when butted up together. The graceful swags on each end, which are trimmed with a fine silk/viscose mix cut fringe, are folded in opposite directions so they hang symmetrically. The curtains themselves are trimmed with a co-ordinating ruched fringe.*

BELOW RIGHT *The deep-buttoned trefoil stool has a long bullion fringe with attached bobbles that tie in with the other trimmings and protect the skirt of the stool.*

BELOW *A selection of antique and reproduction tapestry scatter cushions add character to the room, and break up the solid green of the sofa.*

RIGHT *Yellows and olive greens were the colours picked out for this small but elegant first-floor drawing room of a London town house. The ceiling height is fairly low, therefore it was important to keep the swags of the window treatment shallow in order to let in the light. The curtain fabric is a contemporary damask, and the tails are backed in a ribbed ottoman fabric that has also been used on the three-seater sofa.*

BELOW *A painted reproduction bergère-style chair is covered in a geometric woven fabric with a stitch pattern forming the squares. The upholstery has been neatly finished off with a double row of self-piping. The colours of the chair echo those used in the room.*

TOILE DE JOUY *The most famous cloth printer and dyer in 18th-century France was Christophe Phillipe Oberkampf. He founded a factory at Jouy en Josas near Versailles, in 1760. Oberkampf developed colour-fast dyes and a method of printing using engraved metal roller presses which gave a precise definition to his designs, setting them apart from fabrics printed with crude wood blocks. His earliest chintzes were variations of stripes with sprig motifs and flowing ribbons, which found great favour with the nearby court of Louis XVI. King and courtiers sported these novel new fabrics as waistcoats and dresses. By the 1780s fashion favoured little vignettes of allegorical scenes, contemporary events or romanticised rustic courtships in the style of the painters Watteau and Fragonard. These were printed in single colours, either red in the manner of a red chalk drawing, or blue in imitation of the Chinoiserie patterns on blue and white china. This type of printed cotton was immensely popular by the late 18th century, for both furnishing and clothing, and it became universally known as* Toile de Jouy *after its town of origin.*

RIGHT Toile de Jouy *looks at its best used in abundance. Contrasts of pattern and texture create the interest in this small room, which has a colour spectrum firmly based on the traditional red and cream of a classic* Toile de Jouy. *The wallpaper and matching fabric were printed to order, from an original design. The fabric is 100% linen, making it suitable for both curtains and upholstery.*

TOP LEFT *The generous lined and interlined curtains have puffball headings to add interest to the top, as pelmets would not be appropriate with the low ceiling. This type of heading is particularly good with poles.*

MIDDLE LEFT *A framed scrap of antique* Toile de Jouy, *derived from Fragonard's 1766 painting 'The Swing'.*

BOTTOM LEFT *Scraps of old fabric have been used for this cushion. The cotton check upholstery adds a contrasting note.*

BELOW *Cushions on the* Toile de Jouy *chairs are covered with an Indian cotton.*

LEFT *Neutral colours were chosen for this country drawing room, with touches of maroon red to give a feeling of warmth. The large windows look out onto a beautiful landscape, and it was essential that the window treatment did not detract from the view. Net curtains were chosen both for privacy and to protect furniture and fabrics from the direct rays of the sun. The main curtains are in a fine cotton/linen fabric, edged with a border of red and green cotton check.*

The large sofa is upholstered in a woven linen with a chevron design, and the fabric chosen for the cushions and the footstool is a maroon red crewel-work on a white cotton background. The cushions are bordered and backed with velvet which introduces an interesting contrast of textures.

LEFT *Inexpensive calico was used for the curtains and pelmet in this charming country cottage. The curtains have been given a fullness with a heavy interlining, and the simple pelmet has a pencil pleat heading which adds further bulk and weight to the fabric.*

The sofa is covered in a cotton check and the box ottoman in a hardwearing, plain canvas. Simple dhurrie rugs help add further splashes of colour and break up the expanse of natural coir matting.

ABOVE *The same three-seater sofa covered now with a natural linen throw with a contrast border and a selection of neutral-coloured scatter cushions.*

Throws can be used as here and overleaf, to completely change the look of a room, or as a purely practical measure to protect upholstery from pets and young children.

THROWS AND CUSHIONS *can completely alter the style of a room. The sofa pictured on the previous page has been given three striking new looks.*

LEFT *The indigo and white woven throw with its simple knotted fringe gives the sofa an ethnic look, reinforced with simple blue and white cushion covers. These colours give the room a cool, summery look.*

RIGHT *A rich red cotton throw with embroidered cushion covers in traditional geometric patterns adds warmth and a touch of exotic African influence.*

BELOW RIGHT *With the wool check throw and heraldic, tasselled cushions there is an instant feeling of tradition, solid comfort and warmth.*

STUDIES AND DENS

A quiet room, with books and papers at hand and somewhere to put everything is a welcome luxury in modern life. To encourage concentration, studies should be calm places, sited well away from the hustle and bustle of the kitchen and the family room. A traditional study has no garish colours or bright patterns. There is often a masculine feel to the room – thick, dark fabrics to keep out damaging sunlight and distracting sounds, sober prints on the walls and sensible lighting.

If space is a challenge, a small corner of a hall or bedroom can be turned into a little haven of peace. All you really need is a comfortable chair, a good supply of reading matter and a promise from other members of the family not to interfere or tidy up the scattered papers.

RIGHT *The epitome of a traditional study, in which the colours and textures of fabrics, wallpaper and carpet have been chosen to complement the gold-tooled leather bindings of the books. The full-length curtains are made of mohair velvet, the design stamped, or gauffraged, onto the fabric. The multi-coloured madras cotton bullion fringe, tassels and rope were specially commissioned. The fringe has been sewn onto the curtains at the base to give additional bulk, and onto the leading edges of the curtains. The generous swag and tails of the softly draped pelmet are enhanced with fringing and the proportions emphasised with hanging tassels and a knotted rope trim along the top. The tiebacks are fixed just above sill height, and the proportions of the windows, curtains and bookcase all relate to one another.*

Patterns are introduced in the form of seat cushions and a hearth rug, the images on the walls have been restricted to monochrome prints and portraits that will not distract the eye. All attention is focused on the books and the well-polished mahogany desk.

ABOVE *A sunlit corner of a bedroom in an old Roman palazzo has been transformed into a quiet seating area. The oriental-style wooden bed becomes a sofa with the help of massed cushions piled against the wall, the cushions in the front row are covered with a white quilted cotton. The folding campaign chairs under the window still retain their original fabric.*

Walls and ceiling are covered in the same cotton ticking as the simple curtains. Curved windows always present a challenge – here the curtains have been lifted well clear of the lovely curve, and the simple box pelmet practically disappears into the wall.

LEFT *An awkward space above a porch makes a good look-out point. What little wall there is has been papered in a pale* Toile de Jouy, *that echoes the lovely landscape beyond. Striking blue patterned curtains, enhanced with goblet headings and a knotted rope trim, draw attention to the window, and provide a means of creating privacy and blocking out the light.*

65

DINING ROOMS

The purpose of a dining room is to provide a setting for memorable meals. Whether your preference is for the truly elegant Georgian style, the robust baronial hall or a pretty scrubbed pine country setting, your choice of fabrics is just as vital in setting the tone as is your choice of furniture.

Practical considerations must apply in an environment where food and drink are served and eaten. If the dining room is to be used for everyday family meals, surfaces should be wipeable and floor coverings not too delicate. Seat covers on dining chairs, whether fixed or squab cushions, are best made of a fabric that washes or dry-cleans well. If, on the other hand, you have a dining room that is only used for special occasions, it presents a wonderful opportunity to treat the room like a theatrical set, where you can dazzle guests with dramatic table settings, flattering lighting and wonderful food.

RIGHT *The magnificent great hall at the House of Monymusk in Scotland has all the stone walls and blackened beams necessary for the authentic baronial atmosphere. Tapestries, a hand-painted heraldic frieze and a stag's head adorn the walls, a beautiful antique carpet covers the wood-planked floor, and the chairs are upholstered in a hunting tartan in appropriate shades of muted heather.*

In this type of setting, tapestry wall-hangings are far more appropriate than paintings or prints. It is not only the style and scale of these tapestries that suit the room; their acoustic properties are also much appreciated during lively dinner parties.

RIGHT *This London town house dining room is used predominantly at night. The red and gold colour scheme was chosen to give the room a rich and inviting feeling.*

The curtain fabric is an Italian striped red and gold jacquard, trimmed with a two-colour tassel fringe,and the tails are lined with a red chintz (left). *At night, candlelight reflects off the cut glass of the chandelier, the polished surfaces of the mahogany furniture, and the sheen of the red chintz, giving the room a lovely warm glow.*

BELOW *The beautiful wood panelling is the main feature in this country dining room, and nothing else in the room should distract from it. As the ceiling was low, the curtain treatment was kept simple, with no pelmet. Full blue-green silk curtains that complement the sheen of the walls hang on a wooden pole stained to match the panelling.*

The simple tablecloth is in a cotton check and unlined so it can be laundered. The high-back chairs are upholstered in an understated woven stripe.

RIGHT *The dining room in this London apartment has a simple yet elegant window treatment that does not detract from the fine furniture and glass chandeliers.*

As the room was to be used both by day and by night, the colours had to work well in varied lighting situations. The cream/yellow curtains are an ideal colour for this as they look light and sunny in daylight and shimmer richly by candlelight. A blue and cream braid finishes off and emphasises the edges of both curtains and pelmet.

LEFT *This dining room is in the same home as the study shown on page 62. The wonderful 18th-century mahogany furniture was worthy of appropriately rich and elegant surroundings. The fabric on the walls and at the window is an ochre red Fortuny printed cotton, and both curtains and pelmet are edged with a madras cotton bullion fringe, which adds both richness and weight to the beautiful fabric.*

The dark colours of the antique Ziegler carpet make a perfect foil for the white marble fireplace and and white dado panelling. Delicate gilt scrolls on the mirror and the intricate work on the glass chandelier add their own kind of elegance to the whole.

The setting demands the sparkle of crystal and silver, crisp white table linen and a centrepiece of old-fashioned English roses.

LEFT *A breakfast table in a kitchen needs to be bright and easy to keep clean. This blue and white kitchen has practical but pretty tiles half-way up the walls, and a vinyl flooring based on a Victorian tile design. The chintz used for the softly gathered blinds, table cloth and seat covers was designed for the National Trust and is based on a chintz found at Castle Coole in Northern Ireland. Although this kitchen is in a town house, it has a lovely, fresh, country feel.*

RIGHT *The simplest of tables in the simplest of settings. The unlined, loop-headed curtains hang within the deep window recess, filtering the light rather than blocking it out. The faded colours of the table cloth are perfectly in keeping as a bright, crisp print would jar in these surroundings.*

BELOW *A sunny yellow dining area in a charming cottage on the west coast of Scotland. A thick madras cotton check has been used for curtains and cushion covers. The curtains, hung from slender, unobtrusive poles, provide a welcome degree of draught-proofing in winter. The cheerful yellow walls are a further antidote to winter chills.*

HALLS AND LANDINGS

Halls are about impact and first impressions. If there is room for an extravagant gesture, make it with a wall hanging, a drape or a door curtain. A hall is not usually subject to a great deal of wear and tear, it may be the place to show off a favourite length of fabric that would not be a practical choice for other rooms in the house.

RIGHT *The colours of the walls and curtains were chosen to complement the wood of the staircase and skirtings and to give this large hallway a feeling of warmth and welcome. The wallpaper is a damask design in a warm ochre colour. The curtains, with an attached pelmet, are in a printed cotton linen edged with a bullion fringe. The wing chair is upholstered in an antique velvet, and the contemporary tartan throw ties in with the colours of the curtains.*

BELOW *Dramatic red curtains frame the staircase in this otherwise subdued hall in a London house. Glowing wood panelling and the neutral colours of the carpet, rug and upholstery blend with the tapestry curtain at the window, leaving the scarlet drapes as an undeniable focal point. The heavy glazed cotton double-sided curtains hang in generous folds, held in place with thick, two-tone ropes. The edges are trimmed with a cut fringe for emphasis.*

LEFT *A hall for a warm climate, with tiles underfoot and a billow of cotton lace at the window. The fresco wall decoration echoes the pattern of the tiled floor, and the white, cream and grey colour scheme is unbroken except for a bowl of lemons on the marble side table. The buttoned seat cushion on the cast-iron bench is upholstered in a cotton canvas, and the scatter cushions look as inviting as pillows.*

ABOVE *A trompe-l'oeil tented ceiling over a stairwell has been finished with an extravagant drop of fabric, held in place with matching ropes and small, single tassels. Long windows on staircases can look bare and cold if left completely undressed, and yet the usual option of unnecessary blinds and dress curtains often get in the way. This solution, with the fabric bunched to one side and in a corner, works well.*

BEDROOMS

If a bedroom is not a relaxing environment, then it is not working. This is the place for comfort, for soft carpets or rugs, fluffy pillows, and fresh prints. Bedhangings are a wonderful excuse for showing off beautiful fabrics, not necessarily from a four-poster bed. Curtains can be secured from a corona or a half tester secured to the ceiling or, in a low-ceilinged room, hung from the ceiling itself.

Bedspreads get noticed. Heirloom quilts of antique lace or patchwork, for instance, will probably set the scheme for the whole room. If lace and quilting are not to your taste, then covers that relate to other furnishings, such as the curtains, may be the answer. Beware, however of drowning in a sea of matching fabric.

RIGHT *This contemporary wrought-iron and brass four-poster bed has been dressed with an off-white tergal voile to soften the formal line of the frame, and to tie in with festoon curtains used at the windows. The wallpaper is a blue and cream* Toile de Jouy *style design, and the co-ordinating fabric has been used for the table cloths and bed valances. The quilted eiderdown doubles as a bedspread, and its neutral presence does not detract from the elegant draperies.*

ABOVE *A detail of the tergal voile drapes, showing how they have been loosely knotted around the bed frame and finial, allowing the fabric to fall in natural folds.*

RIGHT *A restful green and white spare room in the attic of a London house has a quaint sloping ceiling. Capitalising on this aspect, the whole room has been treated as a tent. It is a small room, made to seem larger because the wall covering, ruched blinds and table cloths merge into one another. The pretty little sofa and side chair are upholstered with a trellis deign in exactly the same shades of green and white as the main fabric. The bed stands apart, with a crisp white cotton cover, the upholstered ends covered in a bold silk moiré stripe.*

The shape of the room is defined by the white rope trim that follows the corners, skirtings and covings, and edges of the window sills.

LEFT *A welcoming bedroom in an Irish castle with a profusion of patterns and textures. The antique chintz bedcurtains are lined with a pale green silk that matches the foliage on the large floral design. These colours are picked up in the embroidered panels attached to the back curtain and the underside of the blue silk canopy. The sofa is upholstered in a peach moiré silk and the paisley throw, cushion covers, carpet and rugs all echo the pale greens, creams and rose pinks of the chintz.*

ABOVE *An exuberant red and yellow frilled day bed has a canopy in a printed cotton to match the ruched blinds on either side. The curtains, secured to a wall-hung corona, have been edged with a frill and lined with a plain cream. The frilled scatter cushions and skirt are in a bright yellow glazed cotton, the upholstery in a deep cherry red, both picking up colours from the floral fabric used as a bedcover. Even the lampshade is pleated and frilled.*

LEFT *A London town house bedroom gets a breath of country air from a striking floral wallpaper. The outside curtains of the corona are in a printed cotton with a* Toile de Jouy *design. The corona is lined with a striped cotton/viscose fabric that is repeated on the bedspread and working curtains. The heading of the corona is smocked, as are the tiebacks.*

A more practical upholstery-weight fabric on the headboard brings out the touch of blue from the wallpaper.

ABOVE *Behind the half-glazed doors, treated with the same yellow striped fabric as the curtains, a washbasin and vanity unit are concealed. The desk and stool are antiques, the stool retaining its original fabric. A special cut-pile carpet was woven for the house, incorporating the yellows and blues of the colour scheme; it is used in other bedrooms and on the staircase and landings.*

ABOVE *A detail showing the smocked heading used for the dress curtains in the bedroom on the previous page. The painted pole brings out the blue in the wallpaper.*

RIGHT *Practical considerations led to the two sets of curtains. The window wall is set in a slope so the dress curtains are hung on the outer edge, held against the wall with tiebacks. The working curtains, which are lined but not interlined so they will not take up too much space, hang straight in the reveal.*

LEFT *As this bedroom was small, it was important not to let the bed totally dominate the room, so the four-poster bed has a painted finish to give it a lighter feel. The traditional floral chintz used for both curtains and bedspread is bold and bright without being too heavy.*

ABOVE RIGHT *The pelmets are edged at the top with a plain red chintz contrast binding. The base edges are trimmed with a looped, braided fringe that helps to emphasise the gently curving shape.*

CENTRE RIGHT *The lining of the bed canopy and the centre rosette are made of a pale, fresh printed chintz with a small design. The same fabric has been used to line all the bed curtains and pelmets as well as the glazed cupboard doors.*

BELOW RIGHT *The corners of the quilted bedspread have been cut out to fit around the bed posts. The contrast piping is in the same red chintz used for the contrast edging of the pelmets. Here again the solid-colour edging gives definition.*

LEFT *In this small teenager's bedroom, the bed has been placed between the built-in storage units to gain more space. The curtains are in a printed cotton with a pencil pleat heading echoed in the tiebacks The check fabric used on the headboard picks up the reds and greens of the curtain. The draperies over the bed help to define the bed area and soften the straight lines of the wardrobes.*

BELOW *Another variation on the cream and red theme. Here a pretty brass bed is piled with lacy pillows and half-enclosed with lace curtains. A yellow and white wallpaper matches the full-length curtains and the blond wooden floorboards. The cutwork on the bedspread picks up the red motifs from the carpet, and the whole room exudes a sense of calm and light.*

ABOVE *The curtains and bedhead are in a contemporary American linen* Toile de Jouy *design. The duvet and pillow covers are a standard design but a perfect match.*

RIGHT *This blue and yellow bedroom in the same country cottage uses a co-ordinating range of patterned chintzes and wallpaper. Again the bedlinen and table cloths were*

bought separately but tie in well. The lamp was painted yellow to match the wallpaper and the shade was made of a cotton check stuck to thin pleated card.

RIGHT *A fresh, simple blue and white theme is a good choice for this light, bright guest bedroom in a London home. The wallpaper and main fabric are a classic* Toile de Jouy *design. The mahogany chest of drawers that doubles as a bedside table adds a bit of colour and warmth to the room.*

ABOVE LEFT *The padded headboards have ruched borders trimmed with plain blue cord instead of conventional piping.*

ABOVE *A stiff, shaped pelmet is edged with the same cord, applied just above the base to emphasise the attractive form.*

LEFT *The bedspreads are quilted, the style of the quilting following and emphasising the broad stripes. The piped and scalloped edge of the cover is repeated on the overskirt of the bed valance, and the underskirt is in a plain, dark blue chintz.*

RIGHT *A paisley bedcover and a fringed shawl help to establish the stylish comfort of this country cottage bedroom. A crochet curtain hangs from the pole above the window, obscuring the modern radiator behind the bed. The simple, full-length unlined cotton curtain picks up the creams and reds of the casually draped shawl, the warmth of polished pine and the soft white of the lime-washed walls.*

BELOW *A pair of cane beds are given an exotic touch with matching silk embroidered covers evoking Indian crewel-work designs of stylised tropical fruits and flowers. The covers have been trimmed with a heavy bullion fringe to give extra weight and help them drape better. At the window, cheerful tartan curtains hang from a discreet pole that follows the line of the cornice.*

BATHROOMS

The decoration of a bathroom requires more thought than merely choosing tiles and towels. While there may not seem to be a lot of scope in the small modern bathroom for curtains and drapes and dramatic wall finishes, it is amazing what a small touch of imagination can bring to a functional space.

ABOVE *This is a corner of a large bathroom in a castle near Dublin, with inky-blue colourwashed walls and a well-worn stone-flagged floor. An intricate chintz swag-and-tails pelmet hangs over the curtain-less window, turning the deep recess, with its amusing collection of statuary and prints, into a dramatic focal point.*

RIGHT *The all-in-one effect of matching wallpaper and blinds works well in a small space. Here the gently ruched blind has been edged in red for definition. The vinyl flooring picks up the creams and reds of the wallpaper, and the off-white paintwork complements the marble surround of the washstand. The mirror with wall lights helps the room feel wider.*

ABOVE *The authentic look of an 18th-century print room has been cleverly re-created with cut-out prints, borders and tassels stuck to yellow painted walls. The fabric chosen for the curved blind is a heavy, opulent black and yellow design that also evokes the period, and the little cut fringe adds an appropriately witty touch.*

RIGHT *A bathroom with a neatly tailored, masculine air, achieved with smart ochre and black marble-effect panelling and rows of matching prints. The neat roman blind is smartly striped with bands of the same colours. Fluffy white towels on the heated brass towel rail are the only concession to softness and comfort.*

ABOVE *Muslin is a filmy, trasparent fabric with a wonderful feel. Because it is so cheap, it can be used in abundance. These grandly swagged and draped curtains are in keeping with the lovely proportions of this elegant room, yet they are practical – gently filtering light and providing privacy. The round table has a chintz skirt and a white cloth – a treatment normally reserved for the drawing room, but fitting in well here.*

RIGHT *A pretty, flower-sprigged bathroom with ample space for everything. The printed voile blind, with its scalloped edge trimmed with pink, is a match for the wallpaper. The dotted voile curtains have a frilled edge that is repeated on the softly gathered pelmet, and the whole effect of the window treatment is suitably refined and light. The crisp cotton skirt around the pedestal basin adds a pattern of a different scale.*

GARDENS

In the summer months, most gardens become outdoor rooms, with tables and chairs, awnings and umbrellas sprouting up on lawns, patios and balconies. Far too many ranges of garden furniture are covered in garish floral prints that fight with the subtle shades of nature. Plain colours, understated prints and muted hues are far more effective. Deckchair canvas comes in a variety of imaginative designs and colours, including bold checks and stripes that look perfect in a garden setting. This canvas, which has been treated to withstand the elements, is a good choice for garden upholstery and cushion covers, although it only comes in narrow widths.

Garden umbrellas are particularly vulnerable, and the fabric should, if possible, be treated to make it waterproof and rot proof. Umbrellas should always be thoroughly dry before they are stored away for any time.

Garden furniture is best made of natural materials. Wood, cane and painted metal look far better among the trees and shrubs than the more practical plastic. Even for an urban balcony or roof garden, plastic furniture is not always the best choice, as after a few seasons of exposure to city grime, the plastic becomes ingrained with dirt. Choose furniture that is not too heavy to move, as it will certainly have to be put away during the inevitable summer rains.

RIGHT *Pretty cane furniture on an overgrown balcony. A paisley throw blends happily into the background and the cheerful cushion covers add a welcome splash of colour.*

BELOW *A Brazilian wedding hammock, crocheted from thick white cotton, swings enticingly in the breeze.*

LEFT *The geometric shapes of the candle lanterns and the clean lines and curves of the painted metal armchairs are enhanced by the crisp white cloth with its simple stylised leaf pattern. Squab cushions make the chairs a more inviting prospect; they are covered in a sunny yellow cotton fabric, with the self-piping extended at the corners to form ties.*

BELOW *A glassed-in patio with a profusion of greenery makes a wonderful summer sitting room. The upholstered chairs can stay out here all year long. The fabric is a floral print with a light ground, and trimmed with a dark pink scalloped braid. The trailing patterns of the leaves and flowers are a perfect choice for this lovely setting.*

ABOVE *On balmy afternoons and summer evenings, the famous restaurant* Le Manoir aux Quat' Saisons *set in the beautiful Oxfordshire countryside, offers guests aperitifs on the lawn. The white cast iron furniture is a practical choice as it can be left out all year round. It is made more inviting with rose pink squab cushions and matching sun umbrellas, the edges fringed and tasseled in white.*

RIGHT *A table laid for tea in an English country garden. Generous cane chairs and loungers are comfortable enough to while away the whole afternoon. The substantial cushions are covered in an Indian cotton print that has no fight with the roses blooming in the surrounding flower beds.*

A rug on the lawn both defines the seating area and prevents the legs of the table from sinking into the lawn.

The Fabrics

It is the combination of colour, pattern and texture that gives each individual fabric its own personality. Silken velvets and figured damasks, for instance, are timelessly elegant, while white lace and simple floral cottons are forever associated with freshness and simplicity. Fortunately the choice of fabric is enormous, whether it is a contemporary version modelled on a design from the past, or an innovative new weave or pattern.

TAPESTRY

N ow considered superior works of art, tapestries were originally used more for practical than aesthetic reasons. They were made for the wealthy to provide insulation and warmth and to cover up the dull and dirty wall surfaces of their draughty palaces and castles. In the 15th and 16th centuries, although very expensive, tapestries and embroideries were often the only decorative soft furnishings to be had.

The word 'tapestry' refers to a hand-woven fabric, generally made from wool and silk, with a picture woven into it. Designs were copied from a 'cartoon' – a scaled-up working drawing. Most early tapestries were specially commissioned for a particular house and room or bed; sadly few early tapestries have remained in their original locations, as in medieval times princes and nobles moved from castle to castle, taking their wall hangings with them, so they were frequently cut up and refitted. They were normally suspended from rods hung a few inches from a wall.

TAPESTRY MAKERS

Tapestry is frequently confused with embroidery. An embroidery design is worked with a needle and thread onto a finished cloth, while the design in a tapestry is woven as the cloth is being made. Many tapestries took their name from the centre where they were made. Arras in Flanders was the first centre of the industry, so much so that for several centuries the word for tapestry in English was 'arras'. Early designs depicted scenes of court life, meticulously observed hunting scenes, and naturalistic flowers and foliage.

The English produced magnificent wool and silk tapestries from a workshop in Mortlake founded in 1618. The most famous of its works was the *Acts of the Apostles*, copied from the Raphael cartoons. Towards the end of the 17th century, the Soho district of London became an important tapestry-producing area, specialising in popular Chinoiserie designs.

It was not until the 18th century that French centres of tapestry-making, Gobelins and Beauvais, became important enough to rival Mortlake. Many Gobelins tapestries made to furnish the royal palaces of Europe were woven to designs by well-known artists such as Charles Lebrun and François Boucher. The Beauvais centre produced designs largely on classical themes, and the Aubusson centre, which rose to prominence in the mid-18th century, specialised in smaller tapestry pieces, known as *portières* and *entre-fenêtres* and furniture coverings, all woven in Aubusson's characteristic palette of coral pinks and subtle pale colours.

From around 1875 onwards, tapestry-making in England enjoyed a revival thanks to the Arts and Crafts movement. William Morris produced his first experimental piece in 1879 using an 18th-century manual as a guide. The figures were generally to the design of the artist Edward Burne-Jones, while Morris and others created the naturalistic backgrounds. Themes such as the Arthurian legend were favourite subjects, echoing the medieval origins of this art form.

ABOVE *Angeli Laudante, a tapestry worked in wool and silk by Morris and Co in 1894 to a design by Edward Burne-Jones.*

RIGHT *This detail from a magnificent antique tapestry panel is typical of 15th- and 16th-century designs with large, naturalistic foliage and birds. Tapestries age gracefully, and these muted natural dyes have faded beautifully with the passing years.*

TAPESTRY TODAY

The term 'tapestry' is now broadly used to describe a heavy, frequently machine-woven, decorative panel. Some of the designs are replicas of antique patterns, but because of the way they are made and the inclusion of man-made fibres in the cloth to give added durability, they lack the subtle colouring and richly varied designs of those magnificent works of art from earlier periods.

DECORATING WITH TAPESTRY

All the modern tapestries shown on this swatch board are highly suitable for upholstery use. They are particularly appropriate for re-upholstering antique chairs, as long as the pattern is chosen to complement the style and date of the chair. It is also important to make sure the scale of the design is correct; for instance, use larger pattern repeats on settees or high-back chairs where they can be appreciated.

These fabrics can also be used for curtains, in particular for a hall or dining room, or wherever the house cries out for a Medieval style of fabric. They look magnificent but their drawback is expense and weight. Once lined and interlined (which they should be) tapestry curtains will be very heavy, so make sure the curtain track or pole is strong enough to support them. Heavy, stained hardwood poles, or those with a brass or wrought iron finish, look appropriate with this type of fabric. Tapestry also lends itself to pole draperies, or a single curtain pulled to one side of a door or french window. For trimmings, choose textured, heavy-weight ropes or fringes, as anything flimsy will look out of place.

There is a trend for cutting up damaged or worn antique tapestries to make scatter cushions, which certainly add character and richness to a room. The cushion size should be kept as large as possible, or the pattern will be wasted or lost.

1

5

RIGHT *This selection of modern, machine-woven tapestries take original tapestry patterns as their design inspiration. They would look best as upholstery on antique chairs or as magnificent curtains to give a room a distinct Medieval feel.*

1 J. PANSU: *Clermont*

2 J. PANSU: *Fruits de la Passion*

3 RF ROMO: *Aubusson*

4 LELIEVRE: *Tapisserie Carrages Uniques*

5 LIBERTY: *Classic Weaves, Finsbury*

2

3

4

EMBROIDERY

N EEDLEWORK IS AMONG THE OLDEST of handicrafts, and has been practised for centuries all over the world by professionals and amateurs alike. Indeed, it is often difficult to distinguish who did what, as many amateurs were every bit as skillful as the professional workshops. The art of embroidery was not limited to the women of the household – men, women and children from all walks of life enjoyed this gratifying activity. In fact, until the 19th century, it was mostly men who were responsible for the professional work.

Many grand households employed embroiderers whose occupation it was to decorate clothing for both adults and children, and to make furnishings such as bed hangings and cushions. The lady of the house and her family would also be working on fine needleworks, generally on smaller pieces and bed linens. Very grand items, such as the hangings for a state bed, would undoubtedly have been made in a professional workshop; in fact, many of the French silk-weaving factories had their own embroidery departments working on rich silks, velvets and damasks.

TRADITIONAL EMBROIDERY

Early embroideries were worked on a range of background fabrics from silk and cotton to canvas, in combinations of wools and silks. Antique silk pieces are very rare and best kept in museum conditions – it is generally easier to find embroideries made from coarser materials. Examples from the 16th century are generally small panels, with monochrome stylised floral and leaf designs. By the beginning of the 17th century, designs were becoming livelier and more figurative, with animals and naturalistic themes and a greater variety of threads and stitches.

Both professionals and amateurs could buy canvases with designs drawn on them, rather like the embroidery kits available today. If further inspiration was needed, it could be found in a range of printed sources – not all them originally intended for needleworkers – such as books of emblems, natural history and beautifully illustrated herbals. New techniques, such as blackwork (black thread on white) and whitework (white thread on white) became increasingly popular.

Embroidery on canvas was particularly popular for upholstery during the 18th century. It was durable and practical and it is still an attractive treatment for antique upholstered pieces. Early 18th-century designs were similar to those found on tapestries, but on a smaller scale: biblical and hunting scenes, classical myths and floral landscapes were popular. But for most of the 18th century, it was the exquisite depiction of flowers that concerned embroiderers: sprigs and bouquets, sometimes lightly gathered into ribbons with the occasional bird and insect darting about, were the most fashionable themes of the day.

In stark contrast to the elegant and subtle 18th-century embroideries was the style fashionable in the mid-19th century, Berlin woolwork, named after the city of Berlin. Designs were printed in quantity, making full use of the brilliant, even garish,

ABOVE *This fine needlepoint fish is appliquéd onto the satin hangings of a magnificent late 18th-century four poster bed at Blair Castle in Perthshire, Scotland.*

RIGHT *This exquisite silk embroidery hanging is displayed at Standen House in West Sussex. It was designed by William Morris and worked on by Margaret Beale, one of the founders of the Royal School of Needlework, and her daughters in the late 19th century.*

chemically-dyed wools that were then newly available. It was typically worked with big, bold stitches, easy for the amateur, and the subjects were often scenes with children, animals and big, bright flowers. Beads were sometimes incorporated for extra sparkle and richness, and this technique is to be found on cushions, book covers, and a huge variety of Victorian decorative household items.

ART NEEDLEWORK

The Arts and Crafts movement of the mid-19th century gave a great boost to needlework as a decorative art form. Needlework schools were set up to ensure the survival of the traditions of the craft. William Morris, the leading figure of the Arts and Crafts movement, designed embroideries in keeping with his wallpapers, tapestries and fabrics, in lovely muted colours.

By the beginning of the 20th century, sewing machines made mechanical embroidery and beadwork possible and increased their use commercially. But the traditional creative pastime of embroidery in all its different forms is still widely practised, giving many people great satisfaction as they see their works evolve.

DECORATING WITH CREWEL WORK

This form of embroidery, which involves stitching wool onto natural cotton and twill backgrounds, was practised primarily in Britain and North America. The earliest examples are British, dating from the early 17th century, and the typical product was bed hangings. The designs depicted naive birds, animals and flowers, often intertwined with tropical foliage. Many of the motifs, such as the tree of life, were influenced by Indian designs and taken from chintz patterns. American crewel work patterns tend to be less dense and smaller in scale.

Many modern crewel work fabrics are made in India and still bear the influence of Eastern motifs, in particular the Indian palampores and foliage designs which were first imported to England in the 17th century. Crewel work is suitable for all types of curtains, and it can, at a pinch, be used for upholstery, but as the linen backgrounds are usually left undyed, they are not that practical. The fabric cannot be washed as the coloured yarns would run, and even when dry cleaned may cause a problem.

RIGHT *Samples of blue and white crewel work, suitable for curtaining. The large stitching is prone to getting pulled or caught, so I would only recommend it for light upholstery use.*

1 FIRED EARTH
2 FIRED EARTH
3 Tassel by G.P. & J. BAKER: *Divertimenti*
4 COROMANDEL: *Chimar*
5 COROMANDEL: *Butterfly*
6 MARVIC: *Sunam*
7 Braid by BEAUMONT & FLETCHER

2

3

5

6

4

QUILTING AND PATCHWORK

ARLY QUILTS WERE ORIGINALLY MADE as a means of keeping warm in bed. There are accounts of quilts being used to sleep on as well as under, providing both a soft and comfortable base and a warm covering. In essence quilts are made of two layers of fabric joined together with stitching, usually with a soft layer of wadding in between. The technique is common in Japan, India and all over Europe and America.

ABOVE *A finely-stitched reversible cotton and satin coverlet with unusual edging dating from the turn of the century.*

PLAIN QUILTS

There is a strong tradition of quilting, dating back to the 17th century, in France, where quilted coverlets called *boutis* were made of silk and cotton in plain colours. The most elaborate have a fine cord inserted between the two layers which gives an added depth to the elaborate patterns. *Boutis* made as wedding gifts were patterned with symbols of love and good luck, such as hearts, lover's knots, interwoven initials and dates. Examples of quilting on plain white fabric, such as the Durham whitework quilts from the north of England, date back to the 18th century.

BELOW *A striking red and blue early 19th-century Welsh flannel quilt with a centrepiece of appliquéd hearts.*

MAKING PATTERNS WITH PATTERNS

Patchwork quilts first became fashionable in the second half of the 18th century, when the East India Company started importing Indian cottons. Before this time, patchwork was essentially an economical way of using salvaged pieces from worn-out bed-hangings, curtains or coverlets. By the mid-19th century, the fashion for patchwork had declined in the grander households, but it continued as an essential craft in less wealthy homes.

There are two types of patchwork: Appliqué, where the pattern is cut out and laid onto a background piece, and Pieced or Intarsia, where the prime aim is to recycle old scraps of fabric, and the cut pieces are sewn together side by side. At the end of the 18th century, most patchwork quilts were appliquéd with pieces of fabric of all shapes and sizes. Later quilts were more uniform and geometric in style, creating an overall design. In the late 19th century, there was a fashion for 'crazy' patchwork, with combinations of different fabrics such as velvets, silks and satins all sewn together with a thick feather stitching, often in a bright contrasting colour. Elaborate patchwork was a typical feature of the Victorian home, where it was used for cushions and table throws as well as bed quilts.

AMERICAN QUILTS

Patchwork quilting has always been a popular craft in America. The tradition was well-established by the late 18th century, and each community developed its own styles, patterns and colours. Amish quilts, for instance, are made of plain coloured

cottons of a limited palette – green, purple and black – in geometric designs. Pennsylvania Dutch quilts are adorned with traditional European folk motifs of tulips, birds and feathers, usually in bright colours, mainly red and white. In Maryland and Charleston, South Carolina, their French tradition favoured flower-filled, be-ribboned baskets. Early American quilts are far more sought after by collectors than their European equivalents.

ABOVE *A fine geometric pieced patchwork quilt from Wales, typical of the early 19th century, using a variety of cotton fabrics with floral, striped and spotted designs.*

DECORATING WITH PATCHWORK

Today, many patchwork quilts are machine-made and mass-produced for the commercial market. They are purposely kept to specific colour ranges to enable the purchaser to tie them into a particular colour scheme. If you are fortunate enough to own a beautiful antique quilt, then make that the focal point in the room and choose a complementary fabric that will not distract from its beauty. Patchwork specialists will make up quilts from leftover fabrics used elsewhere in the room or, if you are up to the challenge, you can make your own. For added warmth and padding, use a special quilt interliner such as dacron, and a plain, co-ordinated backing fabric so the quilt is reversible. Quilted fabric, such as chintz, can also be used for upholstery.

LACES AND VOILES

T HE DEFINITION OF TRUE LACE is a fabric created not by weaving, but by construction with either a needle or bobbins, using a technique in which threads attached to bobbins are intertwined to form a pattern. Lace originally developed as a form of openwork embroidery: threads would be drawn out of existing cloth and decorated with buttonhole stitch to form patterns. Later the woven support fabric was replaced with a parchment base which would be removed, leaving only the stitched pattern. This was known as *punto in aria*, meaning 'stitch in the air'. Lacy effects are also achieved with netting, which is sometimes overlaid with embroidery, crochet, or even knitting.

LACE FROM ITALY, FLANDERS AND FRANCE

Early lace was made with linen yarn, although silk, plain or gold- and silver-wrapped, was also used. At this time, lace-making was a household craft: the ladies of the house produced fine pieces of work to trim their garments and household linens. Because of its delicate nature, lace was used as a trimming or accessory to clothing rather than furnishing fabrics.

The best early laces were made in Italy, Flanders and France. As lace-makers moved from place to place, the name of particular laces does not necessarily relate to the place of origin. *Mechlin* lace, for example, is the name given to a style of fine bobbin lace, made not only in the Flanders town of Mechlin, but also in Bruges, and Ghent. *Point de Venise* originated in Venice but was often made elsewhere.

MACHINE-MADE LACE

Hand-made lace takes time to produce, so demand was always exceeding supply. Early in the 19th century a machine was invented for producing net onto which patterns could be embroidered by hand, and by 1813 a machine was developed in Nottingham to embroider the patterns. Nottingham lace, mostly made from cotton, was cheaper and more hardwearing than precious hand-made laces. It lacks the gossamer texture and delicacy of antique laces, but there are some fine examples, mostly of shawls, collars, cuffs and handkerchiefs, dating from the late 19th century

Lace as a household fabric is no more practical today than it was in the past. Its chief use is in trimmings or borders, or as decorative, perhaps secondary, curtains in a bedroom or bathroom where it will look fresh and appealing. Laces made from man-made fibres, such as polyester, are slightly more durable, and make attractive bedcovers especially if used with a coloured undersheet or blanket.

FINE COTTON MUSLIN

Muslins are plain weave cotton fabrics woven from very finely spun yarns. They originated in India and were imported into Britain by the East India Company, displacing home-produced fine linens, lawns and cambrics. One 17th-century

ABOVE *These attractive lace curtains form a perfect frame for the picturesque view from this 17th-century Tuscan villa. Their simplicity also ensures that they do not distract the eye from murals painted either side of the window. The gilded tiebacks add a dramatic touch.*

LEFT *A pretty single four-poster bed combines bed curtains made from a modern voile and trimmed with a cotton bobble fringe, with a beautiful antique linen and lace bedspread. The crimson lining beneath the bedspread enhances the fine stitching of the lace work.*

merchant described these amazing new fabrics as 'so fine you can hardly feel them in your hand, and the thread, when spun, is scarce discernible'.

It was not until the late 18th century that the technology for spinning fine yarns in quantity was in place and muslin could be home-produced. The fabric became immensely fashionable for dresses, draperies and curtains. Even at that time muslin curtains were used largely for practical reasons: to prevent people looking in, to obscure unattractive outlooks, and to protect furnishings from harsh sunlight and sooty city air.

Muslin, or voile, is used in much the same way today, for privacy and decoration. Mostly they are simple and undyed in shades of white and off-white. Corded muslins are self-striped, and other decorative muslins have dots or sprigs applied either by weaving or applying flock; printed voiles are also popular. Some companies offer a service printing designs on muslin to match existing fabrics.

DECORATING WITH VOILES AND LACES

These contemporary voiles and laces are both decorative and practical. Use a patterned or printed voile rather than a plain white tergal – they look much more interesting. Voile secondary or dress curtains can obscure an unattractive view and provide privacy without cutting out too much light. For a more decorative look, add a lace trim or a contrasting fine coloured braid or fringe.

Laces and voiles look good around beds, either as bed curtains on a traditional four poster, as a simple hanging over a bed, or as a blanket cover. Muslins can be stiffened with starch or fine casting plaster and creased into dramatic pleats and folds if so desired. Most modern laces and voiles can be either machine or hand washed, which makes them very practical for curtains and hangings, especially when used in towns where dust and grime are hard to avoid.

RIGHT *A selection of patterned and printed voiles, with designs ranging from pretty lace effects to more graphic styles. If voiles are used as secondary curtains, choose a scale and style of pattern to complement the main curtains.*

1 ANNA FRENCH: *Cantata Cotton Madras Lace*

2 PERCHERON: *Havana Voile*

3 PERCHERON: *Fancinilla Voile*

4 NINA CAMPBELL: *Jack's Lace*

5 SHIRLEY LIGER: *Embroidered Sheer*

6 NINA CAMPBELL: *Canasta Lace*

7 SIMON PLAYLE: *Lily of the Valley*

8 BRUNSWIG & FILS: *Summer Cane Lace*

9 SIMON PLAYLE: *La Chasse à Couvre*

10 CELIA BIRTWELL: *Little Animals Voile*

1

10

3

4

5

7

9

8

6

VELVET

ELVET IS A RICH, DENSE PILE FABRIC woven with two warps – the second looped and then cut to form its distinctive, plush pile. The density and weight of velvet varies, depending on its eventual destiny as a fabric intended for upholstery, curtaining or clothing. Early velvets were made from silk.

THE ORIGINS OF VELVET

Velvet weaving originated in the Near East, and the technique was exported to eastern Europe from Alexandria and Turkey. From the Renaissance onwards, Italy became the prime producer of high quality silken velvets. The main centre was Genoa, with Venice, Milan and, to a lesser extent, Lucca and Modena also in the top ranking. Different types of velvet were named for the city of origin even though they were produced elsewhere; thus *Genoese* velvet, a popular choice for bed hangings, became the term for patterned velvet cut with differing heights of pile.

As early as the 15th century, the Italians were experimenting with decorative velvets: some were brocaded with gold and silver thread, some had a raised velvet pattern on a plain satin ground or even on a damask ground, and some had patterns stamped onto the pile with hot metal plates.

A POPULAR FABRIC

Velvet became more and more popular. Cheaper and durable velvets were, and still are, made from wool, cotton (when the final product is known as velveteen), and even from linen. Utrecht velvet, a combination of linen and goat hair pile, was a particularly tough combination, suitable for heavy upholstery.

As upholstered furniture became more common in the 19th century, so did the use of velvet, with deep buttoning to enhance the pile and the sheen. When used as a curtain fabric it was frequently trimmed with elaborate fringing, braiding and gold threads to emphasise the luxurious richness. Printed and stencilled velvets were produced in the early part of this century. Perhaps the most stunning were those created by Mariano Fortuny, the famous Venetian designer who, besides being famed for his pleated silk dresses, also made distinctive printed velvet wall hangings, inspired by his archive collection of Medieval and Renaissance motifs.

CHENILLE

Named after the French word for caterpillar, chenille is a fabric similar to velvet. And 'caterpillar' is a good description of the yarn: originally made of silk, then of wool and cotton, the yarn has a pile protruding all around. It is not cut like velvet, but looped onto the backing like a hooked rug. Chenille yarn was incorporated for its decorative qualities into 18th-century brocades and embroidery, but became popular as a fabric in its own right in the 19th century, when it was used in profusion for table cloths, upholstery and cushions.

RIGHT *A late 17th-century elbow chair from Knole in Kent. It is covered in an original Genoa velvet in a damask style design, and trimmed with a complementary tassel fringe.*

BELOW *This beautiful gilt chair is covered in a crimson silk velvet. The strong, rich colour enhances and complements the gilt perfectly.*

DECORATING WITH VELVETS

Velvets and chenilles are wonderfully rich, luxurious fabrics, suitable for everything from upholstery and curtains to table cloths and cushions. Plain velvets are available in various weights and combinations of natural and synthetic fibres that affect their wearing qualities. Cotton or linen velvets tend to be less shiny than silk or viscose. I prefer chenille, or velvets with a slight texture, for upholstery use as they will not mark so easily. When making up curtains or upholstering a chair, make sure the pile on each piece runs in the same direction, as the way light falls on the pile makes a dramatic difference to the colour.

Velvet can be expensive, but if you invest in a good-quality, hardwearing fabric it will repay the outlay in the end. If your budget does not run to large quantities of expensive velvet for curtains, then you can still add enormous warmth and depth of colour to a room with a velvet table cloth or a few scatter cushions trimmed with a chenille or wool bullion fringe.

Heavyweight velvet curtains look good simply hung from a pole. If you want something more elaborate, choose a deep, simple pelmet trimmed with a fringe, or a stiff, shaped pelmet edged with braid. Although velvet is thick and heavy, it is always advisable to line and interline curtains so they hang better. All velvets must be professionally dry cleaned. Good velvets last a long time, and I think they actually look better with age, rather like leather.

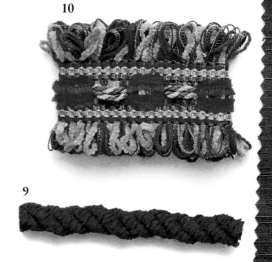

RIGHT *These patterned velvets and chenilles are perfect for upholstery, as plain velvets tend to show marks. Just a few yards of velvet will add warmth and richness to any room.*

1 MULBERRY: *Plantagenet Lampas Chenille*

2 JAB: *Torreon*

3 PERCHERON *Quadrille*

4 OSBORNE & LITTLE: *Pasha Velvet*

5 CHANÉE DUCROCQ: *Ecuriel*

6 OSBORNE & LITTLE: *Palanquin*

7 MULBERRY: *Saladin Chenille*

8 SAHCO HESSLEIN: *Ebro*

9 Chenille cord by WENDY CUSHING

10 Chenille fringe by JAB

2

3

4

7

5

6

DAMASKS AND BROCADES

DAMASK IS A WEAVING TECHNIQUE rather than a fabric. Damasks are generally monotone, woven in either silk, wool, linen, cotton, man-made fibres or a combination of fibres. The characteristic weave pattern is created by the upper and lower faces of the same weave, making the fabric reversible. The name Damask is taken from its place of origin – Damascus – where silken damasks were being produced as early as the 12th century. The characteristic motifs of scrolls, pinecones, paired animals and birds, and exotic flowers and fruits such as pomegranates, are still recognisably Middle Eastern.

FURNISHING FABRIC

Damasks for upholstery were originally made from wool yarn. The fabric was produced in Italy in a limited amount of colours, predominantly shades of crimson and plum. Silk damasks appeared in the 16th century – the sheen of silk is particularly well-suited to this technique since it brings out the pattern – and they adorned the walls and furnishings of fine houses throughout Europe during the 18th century.

Damask was produced in Britain, largely in Scotland, throughout the 18th century in the rich reds and blues that were typical of the period. In America, damasks were originally imported, but later also manufactured there using wool and worsted fibres. Occasionally the distinctive designs were not woven into the fabric but embossed using hot metal rollers or templates.

WHITE DAMASK

In the Netherlands, very elaborate and beautiful linen cloth was woven in the 18th century using the damask technique. The pieces were highly prized as table cloths and napkins. The Irish linen damask industry sprang to prominence when the persecuted Huguenot weavers fled the Netherlands, taking their skills to the source of fine Irish flax. Linen damask only fell into decline when cotton provided a cheaper alternative. White damask table cloths look their best when starched and brought to a high gloss with an iron to accentuate the pattern.

BROCADE

The richest, most expensive and elaborate of all woven fabrics is brocade. Designed to give the impression of embroidery, it is the result of a very complicated weaving process using many colours and threads of silver and gold. The different coloured threads run at the back of the cloth and are brought to the surface where they are needed for the raised and textured pattern. The name is derived from the Latin word *brocare* meaning to figure. Brocading was a term used to describe the decoration of

RIGHT *A traditional style damask copied from an original design and made to look more contemporary with a choice of strong colours. This pattern works well for the grand curtain treatment with its swags and tails complemented by a delicate silk fringe.*

BELOW *A contemporary silk damask with an Art Deco design which is better suited to the black lacquer chaise-longue than a traditional damask pattern.*

fabric by weaving gold or silver threads onto a silk, velvet or damask to embellish and enrich it still further. The figures on brocade might be quite free-form, almost like paintings. The finest antique brocades ever produced were those designed in Lyon in the mid-18th century by Philippe de Lasalle whose work was to be seen in all the royal courts of Europe. He wove beautiful satin hangings brocaded with silk and chenille, depicting wonderfully naturalistic birds and flowers with Rococo swags and festoons. Modern brocades cannot compete on that level.

DECORATING WITH DAMASK

Silk damasks are expensive, but there are some very good copies woven from man-made fibres which will wear well and look just as effective if well handled and trimmed with attractive accessories. Cotton damasks are less shiny than silk or satin and are suitable for upholstering sofas or armchairs in daily use. Real silk damasks are probably best reserved for antique gilt side chairs which are more to be looked at than sat upon. The scale of the design should be selected according to the size of the window or the piece of furniture. In general, damasks look good in houses with generous proportions and tall windows, although some of the smaller designs and pattern repeats will work well on small windows. Damasks can be hardwearing, but always take advice from the manufacturer, as some are definitely only suited for curtains, scatter cushions and table cloths. In general, all damasks should be professionally dry cleaned, but cotton damasks can be hand-washed.

1

10

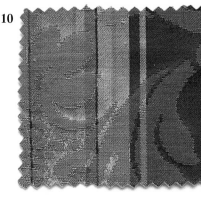

9

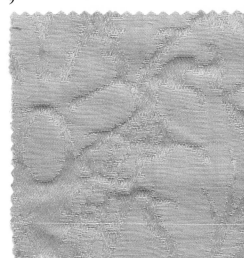

RIGHT *Woven damasks are dramatic fabrics that look their best either as elegant curtains for beautifully proportioned windows, or upholstery on antique chairs. Modern cotton damasks are surprisingly hardwearing.*

1 PARKERTEX FABRICS: *Madrid*

2 DESIGN ARCHIVES: *Manon*

3 G.S.W CO. LTD: *Silk Damask*

4 JAB: *Richelieu*

5 DESIGN ARCHIVES: *Manon*

6 CHANÉE DUCROCQ: *Toscane*

7 Looped fringe by BEAUMONT & FLETCHER

8 HOME COLLECTION/COLLEZIONE ANTIQUES: *Beethoven*

9 G.S.W CO. LTD: *Cotton/viscose Damask*

10 PARKERTEX FABRICS: *Omagh*

2

3

5

4

7

6

DECORATING WITH BROCADES

Traditional brocades are still widely sought after and mainly used for the upholstery of antique furniture. They have a real period feel about them and will consequently look perfect on fine, 18th-century side chairs and small sofas but out of character on contemporary upholstered pieces. These exquisite fabrics are not really appropriate for curtaining, as the designs are traditionally small and delicate. Most brocades are made from silk or silk thread brocaded onto a base cloth, and their texture and sheen comes from the raised pattern on the surface. Good quality brocades are very expensive and fragile but a relatively small amount will transform the look of a fine upholstered piece of furniture as no other fabric could.

When upholstering with brocade, always buy sufficient fabric so the pattern can be centred on the chair, and the back and seat can be matched up. Smaller scraps of brocade make elegant scatter cushions or bell-pulls which look wonderful teamed up with a range of silk trimmings, fringes and tassels. All brocade, like any delicate fabric, should be professionally dry cleaned.

RIGHT *A selection of modern, traditionally-patterned brocades. These exquisite fabrics should not be used in profusion, but enjoyed on a small scale, perhaps as upholstery on elegant 18th-century side chairs and sofas.*

1 Fringe by WENDY CUSHING
2 J. BROOKE FAIRBAIRN & CO: *Coronation*
3 PERCHERON: *Rubelli Zattere*
4 PERCHERON: *Langeais*
5 PERCHERON: *Rubelli Biedermeier*
6 CHANÉE DUCROCQ: *Noailles*
7 Oxford Fan braid by COLEFAX & FOWLER
8 JAB: *Appiano*
9 PERCHERON: *Chotard Batalha*

SILK

THE CHINESE HAVE BEEN PRODUCING SILK ever since about 700 BC and it remained unique to the Far East and eastern Mediterranean until the 10th century, when Spain and Sicily began production, followed by Italy in the 12th century. Silk is a natural fibre taken from the cocoon of the silkworm and then put through a lengthy process of reeling (separating and drying on wheels), throwing (twisting into yarn) and bleaching or dying before being woven into fabric.

COURTLY SILKS

Early silks, originating in the Byzantine Empire and later produced in Spain, were made mainly for the Church or the Courts, and their designs reflect these influences. They became popular with visiting foreigners who were unable to purchase such fine cloth at home. During the Renaissance period a wide variety of beautiful silk fabrics was made in Italy, by then self-sufficient in silk production. Silk was highly prized, and much effort was made to show this shimmering fabric to best advantage with all kinds of complex, innovative weaves and finishes. These silken brocades, velvets and damasks depict designs typical of the period, such as birds, animals, exotic flowers, pinecones and artichokes.

VAGARIES OF FASHION

By the mid-17th century, the silk industry had changed, and France took over from Italy as the leading producer of high-quality patterned silks, using raw materials imported from the East. Designs now followed fashionable furnishing and architectural trends. Mechanisation increased production and the silk industry expanded until the 1760s, when a preference for printed cottons and muslins caused a decline in the demand for silk. However, silk remained the preferred fabric for formal drawing rooms in many of the grander houses. George Smith, who in 1808 published designs for furniture and interiors, stated that 'plain coloured satin or figured damask' should be used to achieve the rich effect necessary for a grand drawing room. Lustred silk, which is taffeta with a high sheen, was also recommended for the lining of bed curtains. Napoleon tried to revive the French silk industry by placing vast orders for luxurious silks for his many houses. French silks of this period favoured a satin weave with repeating motifs in gold or yellow.

SILK TODAY

Many of today's classic patterned silks are reproductions of original designs, created for restoring fabrics in historic houses, and the best quality silks are still mainly produced in France and Italy. Most now contain a percentage of man-made fibre for additional strength and durability, but it is still possible to find the genuine article if you can afford it. The cheapest silks are still those imported from the East, but they tend to be plain or simple woven designs.

ABOVE *Detail showing part of a rich, yellow silk taffeta curtain that has been contrast edged in red and held back from the window by a dramatic brass tieback.*

RIGHT *Plain crimson silk is used to dramatic effect in these flamboyant bed hangings and curtain treatments. The contrast border of gold damask on the bedcurtains gives added drama to the ruched swags edged with heavy gold silk and chenille fringing.*

TYPES OF SILK

The highest quality silk – an exceptionally smooth, bright and shiny fabric – is made from the silk filament which is reeled directly from the silkworm cocoons. Coarser silk yarns are spun using waste from the first reeling, silk from injured or unreelable cocoons, together with filaments from other silk-producing insects. These filaments are spun, like cotton or wool, into a thread. Spun yarn is used to make heavier weight silks, textured slubs and silk mix fabrics.

Moiré silk, which became popular in the 18th century, is also known as watered silk. The rippled effect was produced not by weaving, but by pressing or stamping a heavily ribbed taffeta in order to flatten some of the ribs and leave the others standing. It is the way light reflects on the fabric that causes the effect. Modern moiré silk is passed through engraved cylinders, but the effect may not be permanent – it all depends on the fibres and the way the stamping has been done. Small floral patterns are pressed onto ribbed silk in the same way.

Taffeta is a plain weave silk. In a plain weave, warp and weft are of equal weight. Traditionally, taffetas are finished with a crisp sheen, and although usually plain in colour, they are sometimes printed. They are too thin and lightweight for upholstery and curtaining but make wonderful linings for bed canopies and are ideal for pleated lampshades. Shot taffeta is made by using warp and weft threads of slightly different colours. Mantua silk is an old-fashioned name for a heavy plain weave. Thomas Jefferson ordered crimson mantua curtains for his residence at Monticello.

Satin is a silk with a characteristic smoothness obtained through the weaving method known as satin weave. There are many variations, but basically it is a diagonal weave in which each warp yarn crosses over four weft yarns, then under the fifth, so the smoothness comes from the silk that 'floats' over the other threads. The other side looks the opposite, very matt. Because of the length of the floating yarns, satin is slippery and prone to fraying.

ABOVE *Beautiful plain slub silk curtains dress a full-length sash window. They have the matt look of fine linen. A slub is silk yarn with little nubs or balls of uneven fibre which give the surface of the fabric a slightly textured quality. Compared to many other silks, a slub weave is quite heavy in weight.*

RIGHT *Checks, stripes and spots give a less formal look to an exotic fabric. Patterned and woven silks make beautiful curtains, especially for sunny windows where the light-reflecting qualities of the material can be really appreciated.*

1 JAB: *Rangun*

2 BROCHIER: *Tinta Unita Eucalyptus*

3 SAHCO HESSLEIN: *Emporio*

4 JIM THOMPSON: *Siamese Box*

5 PERCHERON: *Righe Seta*

6 JIM THOMPSON: *Buwan*

7 JAB: *Chopin*

1

2

7

3

4

6

5

DECORATING WITH SILK

Plain, lightweight and printed silks are found in abundance. They are best for curtains and table cloths as their delicate texture makes them unsuitable for upholstery, but they can look stunningly effective, especially in a period setting. Slightly heavier weight raw silks, and those with a slight texture are most appropriate for curtains and maybe light, decorative upholstery, while the heavier silk-based fabrics such as damasks, lampas, brocades and velvets can be used for upholstery as well as curtains and other soft furnishings.

Silk fabrics give a lovely richness to a room. As the light catches the fabric it has an almost three-dimensional effect, and even a single colour will vary considerably with different lighting. When choosing a silk, it pays to look at it in both artificial and daylight in the room where it is to be used, so you can see how it will react to the varied light conditions as well as to the other colours in the room.

All silks are delicate and will require professional cleaning. They will fade if exposed to direct sunlight, so use secondary blinds or curtains, and line and interline all silk curtains to help protect the fabric from damaging ultra-violet rays.

RIGHT *Silk has a wonderful texture, and the subtle patterns of the fabrics shown here enhance all the best qualities of the fibre. These silks have a shimmering, almost three-dimensional feel about them.*

1 JIM THOMPSON: *Buwan*

2 G.P. & J. BAKER: *Kamdi*

3 THE SILK GALLERY: *Demeter/Antique gold*

4 PARKERTEX: *Bengal*

5 JIM THOMPSON: *Pagon*

6 Fan Edging by LIBERTY

7 THE SILK GALLERY: *Demeter*

2

3

6

5

4

PATTERNED WEAVES

IN 1802, THE FRENCHMAN JOSEPH-MARIE JACQUARD invented a loom with a punch card system that was capable of producing multi-coloured, complex designs with different textures. This invention revolutionised weaving, as patterns with intricate curves and scrolls could now be achieved with just one weaver to operate the loom. The Jacquard loom not only speeded up the weaving process but also removed the possibility of errors made by inexperienced drawboys, who moved the hooks to pick up the different coloured threads on the old draw looms.

Jacquard is the general term used to describe patterned woven fabrics such as damask, brocade and lampas – similar to brocade but heavier, and with a figured pattern created by additional coloured warps and wefts, so it is not reversible.

FLORAL SCROLLS

Most of the designs created in early jacquard fabrics were heavy floral motifs in a variety of colours, and they were usually woven in easy-to-handle cotton and worsted fibres. Designs were limited, as only a few designers were capable of producing the punch cards, but the designs that were recorded on cards could easily be repeated over many years. The loom was also found to be capable of producing patterned carpets and 'tapestries'.

Jacquard weaving was introduced into Britain and America around 1810, when M. Jacquard patented a similar process for silk looms. The beautiful and elaborately woven Victorian paisley shawls, which look lovely thrown over a sofa or armchair, were made on looms of this type.

ARTS AND CRAFTS JACQUARDS

William Morris turned to a Jacquard loom to produce the stunning woven fabrics he made in his workshops in Merton, Surrey from 1881 onwards. He employed an old French weaver from Lyon to help him transfer his designs onto the punch cards for the Jacquard loom – a process that required much time and patience. A contemporary visitor described the workshop: 'the hand-looms are working busily, the shuttles flying to and fro between the webs with a speed like lightning ... there are many looms, and beautiful-coloured threads are being woven into beautiful materials on every side'.

For this weaving technique, Morris designed a range of almost heraldic patterns, inspired in part by early Italian examples, many of them centred round the bird motif. The names of the patterns speak for themselves: 'Bird', 'Bird and Vine', 'Dove and Rose', 'Peacock and Dragon'. To add even more to the texture, he combined different yarns of wool, silk and cotton in their weaving.

ABOVE *A contemporary jacquard, incorporating a background stripe and a trailing floral motif. The weight of this type of fabric makes it suitable for heavy-duty upholstery, as well as curtains.*

RIGHT *A woven twill jacquard fabric from the famous 'Peacock and Dragon' design by William Morris.*

DECORATING WITH PATTERNED WEAVES

On this page is a selection of tonal, patterned weave fabrics with a variety of designs of different scales. All are suitable for upholstery, loose covers and curtains. Consider the overall style of your room when choosing a patterned weave – some patterns are bolder and more contemporary than others. You also need to bear in mind the size of the pattern. A small button-back chair, for instance, needs a small-scale design so the overall effect can be appreciated. An unresolved chunk of a large design never works. It is important to match up patterns on back and seat cushions, just as you would for a printed design.

These types of textured fabrics will wear better than plain weaves, as marks will tend to blend into the pattern, and the areas that get most wear, such as headrests and arms, will not develop the tell-tale shine of worn, plain fabric. It would be wise to have these fabrics carefully dry cleaned, although some of them may be washable depending on their fibre content and on whether they have been pre-shrunk – check with the manufacturer if in any doubt.

RIGHT *From pretty little geometric patterns to scrolling stylised foliage, there is a patterned weave to suit almost every taste. These fabrics are subtle and rich, and team up well with printed patterns and plains.*

1 PERCHERON: *Rubelli Abruzzi*

2 OSBORNE & LITTLE: *Sunstich*

3 TITLEY & MARR: *Palma*

4 BEAUMONT & FLETCHER: *Marlowe*

5 JAB: *Newport*

6 Gold looped fringe by BEAUMONT & FLETCHER

7 MANUEL CANOVAS: *Rohan*

8 CHANÉE DUCROCQ: *Rigoletto*

9 JOHN STEFANIDIS

10 BEAUMONT & FLETCHER: *Romanus*

1

3

2

7

4

9

6

8

10

5

DECORATING WITH TEXTURED WEAVES

There is a large variety of patterned and textured weaves available, some containing only natural fibres and some with an addition of man-made fibres for extra durability. The content of the fabric will determine its suitability for the application you have in mind. Some of the textured weave swatches on this page give the impression of being quilted and are therefore very good for upholstery, bedcovers and tablecloths, and they will also hang very well as curtains.

Fabrics with light-coloured backgrounds tend to pick up dirt marks fairly easily, so for sofas and chairs which may get a lot of use, choose a fabric with a darker ground colour. As with the patterned weaves, check with the manufacturer if the fabric is washable; otherwise have it dry cleaned.

All fabrics used for upholstery should have passed the appropriate match and flame-retardancy tests. If they have not, then it will be necessary to place a barrier cloth underneath.

9

RIGHT *Textured weaves have raised patterns, making them very suitable for upholstery as signs of wear and tear and dirt marks are less noticeable than on a flat surface. Some of these floral designs are modern re-interpretations of traditional textured weaves.*

1 PIERRE FREY: *Givacary*

2 SANDERSON: *Home Spun*

3 MULBERRY: *Thistle*

4 Cord *Divertimenti* by G.P. & J. BAKER

5 MANUEL CANOVAS: *Lorca*

6 PIERRE FREY: *Neuville*

7 G.P. & J. BAKER: *Bijar*

8 MONKWELL: *Glendower*

9 Cord by G.P. & J. BAKER

8

1

2

3

4

5

6

7

WOOL

A S EARLY AS THE MIDDLE AGES, woollen cloth of a bewildering variety and type was produced, employing countless numbers of people in its lengthy preparation. The sheared fleece was first washed and then readied for spinning by either carding or combing. Carding produces a soft woolly fibre, whereas combing removes all the short fibres, leaving a thin strong yarn suitable for tightly woven woollen fabrics such as worsted. After spinning come weaving, dying and finishing, or fulling, which determines the final look and feel of the fabric, from baize which is a well-felted heavy woollen cloth, to the finely napped felty finish of broadcloth, used mainly for clothing.

MEDIEVAL CLOTH

It is very difficult to determine what names were applied to what woollen fabrics, but weaving centres throughout Europe were producing their own specialities from quite an early date. Old inventories make it clear that even in the 16th century, wool cloth could be purchased in stripes and checks. There is also reference to painted serge – for example at Hardwick Hall 'eight pieces of woollen cloth stayned with frett and storie' are listed in the household accounts for 1601. These were clearly an economic substitute for expensive tapestry wall-hangings.

RENAISSANCE ONWARDS

After the 16th century most of the preparation processes were carried out by machines and production of all types of woollen and worsted products increased, from felts and moquettes to damasks and velvets. Wool was frequently combined with other fibres including Angora goats' hair, camel hair and horsehair. During the Renaissance period, Florence was the main centre for woollen cloth production, exporting the finished product to the rest of Europe, Africa and Asia. Woollen cloth was often imported, improved upon and exported back to its land of origin.

WOOL TODAY

Patterned woollen textiles, such as tartans and tweeds, were both originally produced for the clothing market, but have now become fashionable furnishing fabrics, both for curtains and upholstery. Textured woollen weaves and patterned weaves such as damasks make wonderful upholstery and curtaining material. Wool is durable, has good insulation qualities and, being full of natural oils, is non-flammable, so it is altogether highly suitable.

RIGHT *This cosy study has been decorated with a variety of contemporary wool tartan fabrics in different weights and colourways. The arms and back of the sofa are protected from wear by tartan rugs.*

BELOW *An elegant 19th-century mahogany settee surprisingly upholstered in a discreet woollen tweed. The seat cushion has a colourful chenille cover.*

DECORATING WITH TWEEDS

Woollen fabrics, although fairly expensive, add valuable warmth and cosiness to a room. They have many advantages, notably that being inherently hardwearing and flame-proof, they are suitable for any use. They also act as good sound barriers and insulators, so if heat loss or sound transference is a problem, wool fabric attached directly to the walls may be a solution.

Tweed goes through phases of being fashionable as a furnishing fabric. The term 'tweed' comes from the Scottish word *tweel* – meaning a heavyweight textured cloth. Legend has it that a London clerk misspelt the word in the early 19th century, and it became tweed from that moment on. Like so many groups of textiles, they are named for the areas where they are made, each locality producing tweeds with a different look, such as Scottish, Harris, Cheviot, Irish, Yorkshire, Saxony and West of England. Traditionally the wool was locally dyed with natural dyes. Some come in solid colours, some in heathery shades, others with stripes and checks.

Owing to its inherently 'country house' look, tweed is rarely seen in abundance, but nonetheless a touch of tweed can provide a certain chic style to a room. These fairly subtle tweeds would look good as upholstery on a favourite armchair with a complementary woollen throw. Tweeds should be trimmed with subtle, colour-matched braids.

RIGHT *Tweeds are mostly associated with sensible, outdoor country style clothing. But their subtle checks and weaves can look very smart as a furnishing fabric. The wonderful, natural colours would blend beautifully with other fabrics.*

1 RALPH LAUREN: *Devon*

2 THE ISLE MILL: *Glen Tilt*

3 Looped fringe by BEAUMONT & FLETCHER

4 RALPH LAUREN: *Tudor*

5 RALPH LAUREN: *New Market Tweed*

6 THE ISLE MILL: *Glen Carron*

7 THE ISLE MILL: *Glen Keith*

8 RALPH LAUREN: *Staffordshire Herringbone*

9 RALPH LAUREN: *Wetherby*

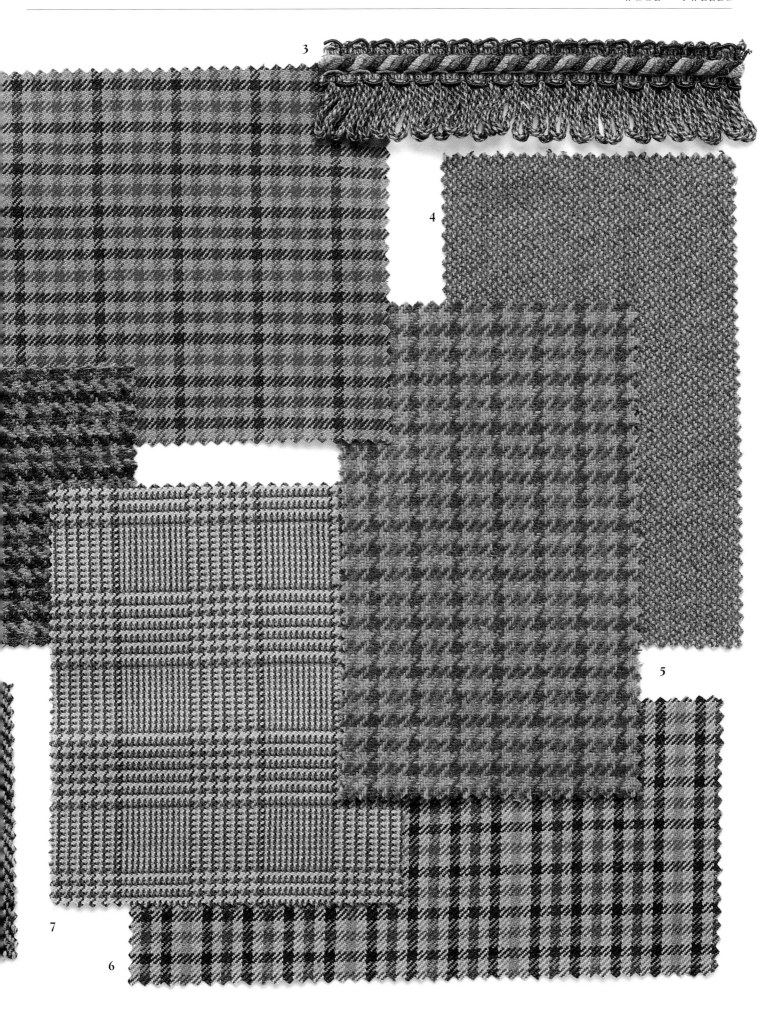

DECORATING WITH TARTANS

Early tartans were woven from woollen yarn dyed with plants and lichens which gave the weavers a palette of soft ochres, madders, yellows, whites and greens. Weaving tartan was a cottage industry and, as only small quantities of yarn could be dyed in one batch, there was a lot of variation in the colourings.

Traditional tartans go back many generations. They evolved as patterns to be worn only by members of a certain clan or regiment. The popular Black Watch tartan, for instance, was introduced by the first Highland regular regiment in 1740. After the Jacobite Rebellion of 1745, tartans and their clannish associations were forbidden by law, and although the law was repealed later in the century, it was not until George IV made a much-heralded visit to Edinburgh in 1822 that the Scots started taking a new pride in their historical tartans, to a certain extent re-inventing them. Queen Victoria's passion for Balmoral boosted their popularity still further. The decoration of Balmoral, finished in 1855, included tartan-covered walls and upholstery, and tartan carpets, and it influenced a whole generation of Scottish hunting lodges and castles. During this period, some clans adopted two tartans – a hunting tartan in predominantly greenish camouflage colours and a dress tartan including a lot of red, which looked bright and cheerful for social gatherings.

Like Queen Victoria, I think tartans look best in profusion. Their rich, warm colours and textures create an inviting, informal atmosphere, especially in studies, libraries and men's dressing rooms. Tartan fabric can be stretched onto walls, made up into simple curtains and used as upholstery fabric. The final touch is to use contrasting tartan rugs as throws on chairs and sofas.

There are many contemporary tartans to choose from. Some are copies of originals with romantic or bloody historical associations, and others are new designs with brighter colours and wilder checks, so all tastes can be catered to.

RIGHT *Tartans with the soft muted colours of natural dyes are the best for curtaining and upholstery. Brighter coloured tartans can be used for cushions and throws.*

1 THE ISLE MILL: *Hunting Stewart of Appin*

2 RALPH LAUREN: *Harrigan*

3 TITLEY & MARR: *Hunting Cameron*

4 THE ISLE MILL: *Cameron of Locheil*

5 ANTA: *John Macnab*

6 ANTA: *Neil Gunn*

7 MULBERRY: *Woven Plaid, Beaufort*

8 MULBERRY: *Ancient Tartan*

9 Looped fringe by BEAUMONT & FLETCHER

PRINTED COTTON AND CHINTZ

EUROPEANS WERE ENTRANCED BY THE COLOUR-FAST, brightly-coloured Indian printed cottons imported by the East India Company. These fabrics, known as *pintadoes* or chintz – the Hindi word *chint* means coloured or variegated – with their interesting colours and opulent designs, looked to 17th-century eyes as if they had been embroidered. The traditional designs were outlined onto the fabric by hand and the colours, made with dyes fixed in a way unknown to Europeans, were hand-blocked on top, sometimes on a dyed ground. Early *pintadoes* had a definite oriental look to the designs, but it was not long before enterprising merchants sent out traditional western patterns for their suppliers in India to copy, resulting in increased sales in Europe.

A PRINTING REVOLUTION

By the end of the 17th century, European printers were working hard to imitate these 'chintzes' which were posing such a serious threat to their trade. Early European printed cottons were not at all elaborate in design. Simple stripes were popular and the fabric was mainly used for clothing. The introduction in 1752 of copper plate printing allowed for more intricate designs to be produced. Hand-block printing, although still used for elaborate, multi-colour designs, was both laborious and somewhat inaccurate. The first copper plate designs were monochrome – generally blue, crimson or sepia designs on a white ground. Although this style of printed cotton was originally produced in Ireland, it became famous as *Toile de Jouy* after the French factory at Jouy near Versailles, where the technique was perfected.

The real advance came with cylinder printing, which speeded up the whole process and made it possible to introduce designs with a number of colours, each of which had to be printed separately and accurately superimposed on the base cloth. Cylinder printing came into general use for furnishing fabrics by about 1815. The first half of the 19th century was marked by continuous experimentation and improvement in fabric printing techniques. New colours, derived from mineral rather than vegetable sources, were developed, producing a brighter, brasher palette. Although floral designs have nearly always dominated the printed cotton market, there were also a wide range of 'pictorial prints' available, depicting anything from cockfighting and Chinoiserie to landscapes and battle scenes.

GLAZED COTTON

In the early part of the 20th century, many of the best-loved designs were copies of earlier ones, favouring stripes, swags of flowers, ribbons and garlands. Today, cottons are either cylinder printed or screen-printed on flat beds – an even more flexible

ABOVE *A modern blue and white* Toile de Jouy *fabric is used to decorate this bedroom in a house in America. The blue paintwork and painted floor give the room a country feel and bring out the blue of the fabric.*

RIGHT *The chintz used in this bedroom was designed by David Mlinaric in association with the National Trust. The design is influenced by the traditional chintzes frequently used in country houses.*

method enabling designs to be modified with ease. Screens are now so easy to set up that elaborate designs can be printed easily and relatively cheaply, and a virtually endless array of colourways can be produced with little trouble.

Today, we generally refer to glazed printed cottons as chintz. Cottons are glazed in order to give the colours depth and to make the cloth more practical, as dust does not cling so readily to a shiny surface. Originally this was done by painstakingly rubbing the surface with a roller, but nowadays a special coating is applied.

DECORATING WITH SMALL PATTERNS

These printed cottons are all contemporary fabrics with a mixture of glazed and flat finishes. Small-scale patterns look good on their own as curtain material for small windows, or as an edging or contrast lining to a complementary larger pattern. They are effective for decorative accessories, such as covers for squab cushions. Typical applications for patterned cottons such as these would be as lining for bedcurtains, for bed valances, or borders on headboards. In general, they look more at home in bedrooms than in sitting rooms, halls or dining rooms where more impact is required.

Fabrics with glazed or resin finishes should be dry cleaned, although this process will eventually diminish the glaze. Only pre-shrunk, 100% cottons printed with run-resistant dyes can be washed, and even so it is always wise to test a small piece before committing a large quantity to soap and water. If curtains are lined and interlined, they should always be dry cleaned, no matter how washable the individual fabrics.

ABOVE *A stylised floral pattern has been used here for a squab cushion. The plain blue piping makes the cushion look crisp and smart – just right for a dining chair.*

RIGHT *Small-scale stylised floral designs, like many of the samples shown here, give the impression of an all-over pattern because it is hard to see where the pattern repeats. They will co-ordinate well with both bolder patterns and plain fabrics*

1 JEAN MONRO: *Lizzie*
2 MRS MONROE: *Featherberry Greens*
3 TRYED TEXTILES: *Peppercorn*
4 TRYED TEXTILES: *Oak Leaf*
5 JEAN MONRO: *Cranford*
6 PIERRE FREY: *Fleurs de Mai*
7 ZOFFANY: *Window Book*
8 ZOFFANY: *Meadow Flower*

3

1

2

8

5

6

7

4

DECORATING WITH BOLD PATTERNS

The designs of these large-scale printed cottons are mostly taken from historical archives and modified to suit today's printing techniques. Coloured and slightly textured grounds give these striking designs added warmth and depth, and it is common to find several choices of colourway in any one design to suit individual tastes and applications.

When making curtains using fabrics with a large-scale designs, ensure that the windows are large enough to cope with the repeat, and that the two curtains match up. There is certainly more wastage with large-scale patterns, but left-over fabric can be turned into cushion covers or perhaps a patchwork quilt. The same considerations apply to pelmets. Pick a style, whether stiff, or soft and gathered, that will complement the pattern and enhance it. Boldly printed fabrics look good contrast-bound with a plain colour taken from the design or from a complementary fringe or rope trim.

Printed cottons are suitable for upholstery, but will not wear as well as a heavier-weight woven fabric, and marks will be visible on lighter backgrounds. Chintzes are popular for loose covers, and it is practical to have two sets made, one in a heavier weight for winter.

RIGHT *These are certainly fabrics with impact, and the strong shades of ochre and terracotta will give a room welcoming richness and warmth. Bold patterns of the same style, 7 and 8, for instance, or 3 and 4, can look very good together.*

1 Tassel by LIBERTY

2 WARNER FABRICS: *Sedgewick*

3 G.P. & J. BAKER: *Palma*

4 MARVIC: *Parterre de Roses by Henrietta Spencer-Churchill*

5 COLEFAX & FOWLER: *Colmar*

6 JEAN MONRO: *Les Pecheurs*

7 DESIGN ARCHIVES: *Goa*

8 MULBERRY: *Medieval Alphabet*

DECORATING WITH FLORAL CHINTZ

Traditional chintzes look right in practically every room of a country house, from bedrooms to drawing rooms. For a slightly grander, more formal look, choose a plain silk or damask for the curtains and introduce chintz as chair covers or table cloths and cushions. It is wise to choose the chintz pattern first and then select the other fabrics and the wall colour with the chintz as a colour guide.

These delightful, old-fashioned chintzes will create an instant, lived-in atmosphere. Today it is not necessary to wait for a fabric to age gracefully, as many are designed in lovely faded colours to look elegantly worn. When choosing a chintz with a large design, check a long length of the fabric, and hang up a loosely gathered piece to get an idea of the way it hangs. Made-up lengths can look very different from small flat samples in a pattern book.

RIGHT *The background colours of these traditional chintzes are predominantly a creamy beige that will co-ordinate well with other fabrics and paint colours. Chintzes with a crisp white ground look wonderful, but are not very practical for upholstery.*

1 MULBERRY: *Floral Bouquet*

2 Fringe by BEAUMONT & FLETCHER

3 JAB: *Kimberley*

4 MANUEL CANOVAS: *Les Petits Coquins*

5 COLEFAX & FOWLER: *Caroline*

6 PERCHERON: *Kasbah*

7 MRS MONROE: *Patricia*

8 MRS MONROE: *Vibernum*

9 Ribbon (discontinued)

1

3

2

4

5

6

7

8   9

DECORATING WITH BOLD CHINTZES

Large, bold chintzes such as these, with dramatic designs on crisp white backgrounds, are ideal for light rooms and sunny climates, but they can look rather stark – on their own they will not create a welcoming and cosy atmosphere. To add more warmth, choose a patterned wallpaper in predominately warm colours and pick out reds, ochres and yellows from the design for paintwork and accessories such as cushions, throws, footstools and lampshades.

The light backgrounds of these fabrics make them impractical for upholstery – unless for a purely decorative or little-used side chair. An interesting application for this type of design, and one which looks stunning, is to have the fabric made up into dramatic bedspreads or table covers and outline quilted so the stitching complements the pattern. The boldness of the colours and patterns invites the use of equally bold and imaginative trimmings.

RIGHT *An outline-quilted bedspread and headboard made from a wonderful, boldly-patterned cotton. The bold swirls and stripes have been teamed with a co-ordinating check.*

FAR RIGHT *These exuberant fabric patterns, based on botanical drawings of fruits, flowers and foliage, would look good at the window of a sunny room leading out to a garden.*

1 LIBERTY: *Flores Botanica Augusta*

2 MRS MONROE: *Rhododendron Sprig*

3 Tassel by G.P. & J. BAKER

4 COLEFAX & FOWLER: *Arabella*

5 ZIMMER & ROHDE: *Fritilla, designed by Charles Sorel*

1

3

2

5

4

LINENS

ODAY THE TERM 'LINEN' is mostly applied to household accessories such as sheets, table cloths and napkins, but linen was once the only woven fabric in the world. It is produced from the flax plant which flourishes in damp soil, and was first known in Egypt, where it grew in rich river silt on the banks of the Nile.

TEXTURE AND WEIGHT

As a woven fabric, linen is much stronger than cotton, although less manageable as a yarn. It proved difficult to weave on power-operated looms, so by the late 18th century, cotton had superseded it as the ubiquitous household fabric. But linen's hardwearing and draping qualities were still prized, and it remained a popular choice for bed hangings and loosely draped covers for furniture. Linen loose covers were primarily used for the protection of expensive silk damasks which were only revealed in their full glory on special occasions. Known as 'loose cases', these linen covers were not made taut and fitting like modern loose covers, and the tapes, strings and bows that attached them were clearly visible. It is a style of upholstery that is now considered quite avant-garde.

Jute and hemp, coarser yarns but with some of the qualities of flax, were considered the poor man's linen, and were made into heavyweight cloth for many everyday household items. They were also used to produce interesting printed textured fabrics for curtaining and wall hangings.

A natural fabric, linen is durable, practical and absorbent, and although it does crease easily, it hangs beautifully. It is ideal for sailcloths, ducks and canvases – the types of fabric where weight is needed – and its textured look was particularly prized in the Arts and Crafts period. By the end of the 19th century, when the Arts and Crafts movement was at its height, linen was considered the perfect fabric for the furnishing of country houses and cottages, and companies such as Heal & Co produced ranges of linens in soft muted tones to complement the plain oak furniture and traditional pottery with natural glazes.

PRINTED LINENS

Linens have been printed for many centuries. Some of the earliest recorded examples are basic, one-colour, hand-blocked lengths used for wall hangings, and hand-painted linen panels made in cheap imitation of tapestries. Today, more printing is carried out on linen-mix fabrics than on pure linens, largely due to expense. Linen is considerably more expensive than cotton and man-made fibres, but its fine qualities add an enviable texture and weight.

RIGHT *In this bedroom at Wightwick Manor, the William Morris printed linen fabric, 'Cray', has been used for both bedcover and curtains. The design and the colour complement the oak panelling. The paintings on the panels are copied from well-known works of the pre-Raphaelite painter, Dante Gabriel Rossetti.*

DECORATING WITH FADED FLORAL LINENS

Linen is suitable for both curtains and upholstery. The designs of printed linens are often very similar to those of printed cottons and chintzes, and some companies will print on both fabrics so the same design can be used for linen upholstery and cotton curtaining. Linen basecloth can be made in different weights and textures which will determine the overall look of the fabric. Pure linen does tend to crease easily, so it is often mixed with man-made fibres.

When choosing a pattern, the scale should always be in keeping with the size of the windows or the piece of furniture the linen will eventually adorn. When upholstering with prints, the central motif should be placed in the centre of the sofa or chair.

The popularity of the understated, faded-look printed linens made by Bennison has never diminished, and now there are plenty of copies. Together with antique furniture, richly-coloured worn rugs and wood panelling, the effect can be genuinely 'country house'. Linen fabrics will add more warmth to a room than a shiny chintz, and in my view linens are more masculine – perhaps because the colourways tend to be richer and have more depth.

Floral linens can be enhanced by adding contrasting borders, fringes and ropes. Although linen is heavier than cotton, linen curtains should also be lined and interlined as it will make them look and hang better. Curtain tracks or poles and their fixings should be strong enough to take the weight of heavy curtains. Linen furnishing fabrics must always be dry cleaned.

1

9

8

RIGHT *These beautiful faded printed linens will enhance schemes both traditional and modern. The lack of definition blurs the edges of the designs, so there is nothing to fight with other patterns and textures.*

1 BEAUMONT & FLETCHER: *Baroque Floral*

2 BEAUMONT & FLETCHER: *Foxglove Garden*

3 BENNISON: *All-over Floral*

4 Tassel by LIBERTY

5 COLEFAX & FOWLER: *Osterley*

6 RALPH LAUREN: *Knightsbridge*

7 PERCHERON: *Rubelli Devonshire*

8 Braid by BEAUMONT & FLETCHER

9 Looped fringe by BEAUMONT & FLETCHER

7

2

3

4

6

5

DECORATING WITH BOLD PRINTED LINENS

The designs of many contemporary printed linens are taken from historic archives. Most of the original designs were hand blocked, and the natural dyes then used were necessarily limited in colour. Contemporary reproductions are not exactly faithful to the originals, as the colours are much stronger and the effect less subtle. Today's fabrics are more colour-fast, and they do not mellow as they once did – shades of green especially were prone to fading to yellow. Strongly-coloured prints can dominate a room and become focal points in themselves – they could detract from other items in the room such as a beautiful antique rug or an attractive oil painting.

Large, bold designs will probably have many colours within them, so start with the fabric and then decide which colour or colours to pick out for other furnishings and wall colours. These choices will determine the atmosphere of the room. Picking out a red, for instance will make the room seem smaller and cosier; a blue will make it fresher but colder and a shade of yellow or green will feel lighter and airier.

RIGHT *A wall hanging showing the full width of a border-printed linen. The fabric is designed to be hung as a panel, horizontally, as here, or vertically, but it could also be used to upholster a sofa. The table cloth and cushion cover are in a fabric from the same collection.*

FAR RIGHT *Linen has a canvas-like texture, so figurative designs appear almost painted on with a soft brush. On cotton, the same prints would stand out crisply and demand attention.*

1 PIERRE FREY: *Quai Voltaire*

2 L. RUBELLI: *Josephine*

3 NOBILIS: *Collection Fontan Giammaican*

4 SANDERSON: *Antique Rose*

5 PERCHERON: *Toile Fronsac*

1

2

3

5

4

CHECKS

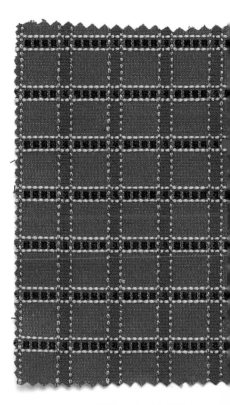

CHECKED AND STRIPED FABRICS are enduringly popular and it seems there is a never-ending supply of new designs available, whether printed, woven or a combination of both. Checks make wonderful co-ordinating fabrics, as there is always one to be tracked down that will tie in with a main fabric, and they look good on their own for everything from lightweight curtains to heavy upholstery and decorative accessories such as cushions.

Checks have an informal feel about them – they can look pretty and fresh in kitchens and gardens, and seriously smart in sitting rooms. They co-ordinate with so many other fabrics, especially more checks, and as they come in every possible scale from tiny pinpoints to huge windowpanes, there is a lot to choose from. The main problem with checks is making sure that the pattern matches and that all the lines are kept straight without stretching the fabric too much. There is no easy way to achieve this – the secret is sheer perseverance.

Printed lightweight cotton checks are only suitable for upholstering pieces that are seldom used. Some cotton checks may be washable, but it is possible, especially with cheaper fabrics, that colours may run, so it is advisable to test a small piece first. Woven checks should be dry cleaned; if the fabric has been Scotchguarded or flameproofed, ensure that these treatments can withstand the cleaning process. Checks can be trimmed with plain, coloured braids or a multi-coloured fringing that picks up colours from the fabric.

RIGHT *Checks can be simple or incredibly complex, but with all woven checks, the different coloured yarns of the weave become apparent, and this is what gives checks their simple charm.*

1 ZOFFANY: *Compendium Checkers*
2 PARKERTEX: *Belagio*
3 Braid by G.P. & J. BAKER
4 Wall tape by COLEFAX & FOWLER
5 PARKERTEX: *Varese*
6 IAN MANKIN: *Regent Plaid*
7 PIERRE FREY: *Marius*
8 LIBERTY: *Onslow*
9 MALABAR: *Mysore*
10 LIBERTY: *Portman*
11 PERCHERON: *Rubelli Mer du Nord*

10

11

1

2

4

5

3

7

6

8

9

STRIPES

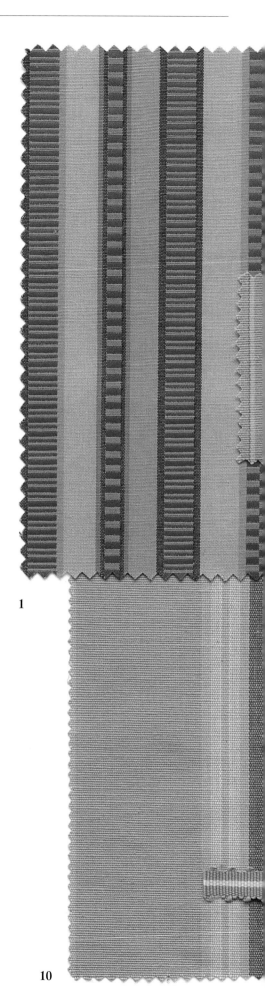

STRIPES AND CHECKS GO VERY MUCH HAND IN HAND and the two are often woven or printed to co-ordinate with one another. Striped fabrics make good curtains, they are easier to handle than checks or bold patterns and not so dominant. In fact, stripes can be quite subtle: many floral or stylised patterns have a discreet stripe in the background.

Ticking is the simplest form of striped fabric, with a thin, single colour stripe on a natural cotton background. It is cheap and can look really striking made up into generously swagged curtains or simple drapes. It has a light ground, so marks will show, but it can be washed.

Printed stripes can be found in a huge variety of patterns, colours and weights, often designed to tie in with more complex patterns. They also look good on their own or as linings and trims for bed hangings or curtains. Woven stripes look particularly good on upholstery and on walls – as long as the stripes are kept straight.

The scale of a stripe should always match the piece of furniture or the window for which it is intended. For pelmets, the fabric can be turned to run horizontally to form a border. Striped moirés are suitable for antique pieces and look wonderful teamed with a plain moiré fabric.

RIGHT *The selection of stripes shown here runs the gamut from simple bands of colour to complex textured and patterned panels. Stripes look good trimmed with a two colour fringe in the same colourway.*

 1 LIBERTY: *Jessam*
 2 Fringe by G.P. & J. BAKER
 3 MALIBAR: *Shalimar*
 4 FIRIFISS: *Romney 5*
 5 PIERRE FREY: *Tisse Tolede*
 6 G.P. & J. BAKER: *Summer Stripe*
 7 RALPH LAUREN: *Marie*
 8 Braid by COLEFAX & FOWLER
 9 JAB: *Lazavo*
10 MONKWELL: *Maypole Stripe*

PAISLEYS

THE BASIC MOTIF OF THE PAISLEY PATTERN derives from traditional Indian textiles – it is like a leaf with a curled and pointed end. The origin is obscure but it has been thought at various times to be based on the pinecone, the palm, the almond and the cypress. It came to be fashionable as a motif on embroidered Kashmiri shawls, made popular by Queen Victoria. The embroidery was imitated by weavers using Jacquard looms, and the design gained its name from the Scottish town of Paisley, where exquisite woollen shawls of fine quality were woven. A paisley shawl makes a distinctive throw for a sofa or a chair, but it does not have to be an original – a metre or two of one of the fabrics shown here, plus a few yards of silk fringing, can duplicate the effect. Many of the original paisleys were made for the fashion industry, and later became popular as furnishing fabrics – now, like any other distinctive design, they go in and out of fashion.

Traditional paisleys are woven in fine wool, and incorporate the colour red. Today, many paisleys are printed, and some of the designs incorporate very un-traditional stripes or border designs. The dark, subtle pattern makes paisleys, large or small in scale, eminently suitable for all types of soft furnishing. The weight and quality of the fabric will determine whether or not it is suitable for heavy-duty upholstery, but it is a good choice, as the dark ground will not show up marks.

RIGHT *Of all these paisley designs, the most traditional is 4 – an intricate swirling pattern of reds, yellows and greens. The paler paisleys have a much more contemporary feel.*

1 Chenille tieback by WENDY CUSHING
2 MULBERRY: *Paisley Stripe*
3 D.G. DISTRIBUTION: *Wellington Stripe*
4 FIRED EARTH: *Paisley woven*
5 Chenille fringe by WENDY CUSHING
6 RALPH LAUREN: *Tatiana (Brasserie Stripe)*
7 MANUEL CANOVAS: *Hayderabad*
8 JAB: *Nimes*
9 CHANÉE DUCROCQ: *Baroda 06*

3

4

2

5

6

7

TRIMMINGS

The word 'TRIMMINGS', or the more attractive French term *passementerie*, encompasses the huge variety of accessories used to embellish and enhance soft furnishings. Braid, tape, fringes, gimp, laces, ribbons, tassels and rosettes can all be included in this category. Their original, practical purpose was to disguise the joins between narrow widths of woven damasks and velvets adorning walls, beds and alcoves in Medieval times. The beautifully worked braids and ribbons were soon used for embellishment as well as disguising seams.

Fringes had a practical beginning too. The end warp threads of a woven cloth were knotted to stop them from unravelling. This simple fringing is still used on cheap table cloths, throws and rugs. More complex fringes evolved from these humble beginnings, complete with their own headings so they could be attached to a piece of furniture, a curtain or a cushion.

A CRAFTSMAN'S SKILL

Trimmings were made from a variety of fibres, particularly wool and silk twined with gold and silver threads that were sometimes tied around a wooden shape. It was a lengthy and expensive process, requiring a lot of expertise. Skilled craftsmen in France and Italy were kept busy making matching sets for individual rooms in royal palaces and grand houses throughout Europe.

By the mid 18th-century, trimmings were immensely rich and intricate, and in grander homes they adorned every piece of upholstered furniture, and beautiful silken fringes and tassels hung from every swag of curtain. The Victorian taste for trimmings was for the over-sized and over-gilded, and by the mid 19th-century trimmings were machine-made and a great deal less elegant.

SUBTLE AND BOLD

Braids, ropes and tiebacks have changed little in basic design over the centuries and, as with many other antique styles, original designs are now being copied, re-worked and re-coloured to bring them in line with today's trends. The great debate is whether trimmings should be subtle and match the fabric, or make a bold statement in sharp contrast. In my opinion, there is room for both views – it depends entirely on individual taste and the style of room. A simple pair of plain curtains can be subtly embellished with a two-tone fan edging, but on the other hand, elaborate swags and tails adorned with tassels, fringes and rope can look wonderful in the right setting.

There is an enormous number of standard ready-made accessories, but it still never ceases to amaze me just how difficult it is to find that perfect match for the fabric in question. Fortunately there are some first rate companies specialising in individual commissions and reproduction work. Hand-crafted *passementerie* is, unfortunately, very expensive and takes a long time to make, but such pieces will give endless pleasure and last for generations.

ABOVE *A magnificent pair of braided and tasselled bell-pulls hang on a simple white wall, a decoration in themselves.*

RIGHT *These tapestry curtains have been given a suitably Medieval feel with a richly decorated tassel and rope tieback worked like a crown with golden threads. The insets have been made to look like a circlet set with creamy-white pearls and glowing rubies. Even the rope has been disguised to look like a string of precious beads.*

BELOW *A beautifully worked tieback embellishes a creamy damask curtain at Victoria House in Portland, Maine.*

THE VARIETY OF TRIMMINGS

Trimmings greatly enhance the look of all soft furnishings. They add richness, finesse and wit to a room and, although expensive, will always get noticed and admired. There are plenty of standard ranges available, in a vast selection of weights, colour combinations and styles. With perseverance it should be possible to find something that will match or tone with the chosen fabric and suit the practical application.

Select the type and scale of trimmings to suit your overall design. I recommend choosing a similar type and weight as the fabric. For silk curtains and pelmets, for instance, a silky viscose tassel or cut fringe would be more appropriate than wool bullion. On the other hand, a large, deep sofa covered in chenille would look strange with a light, silky fringe.

All trimmings are delicate and need to be treated with care. I would not recommend them for family rooms or anywhere that they could be subjected to unintentional abuse. There is one exception to this – around the base of a sofa or armchair, a simple fringe will help prevent the skirt getting kick marks from shoes, and it is certainly cheaper to replace the fringe than to re-upholster an entire piece.

RIGHT *These trims and tassels would enhance the look of pale creamy silks, or the golds and blues of a delicate damask or brocade. These are the colours and weights to choose for edging a textured linen with a pale ground colour, or for bringing a touch of drama to a generous swag of a cheap fabric such as cotton canvas.*

A selection of pale, subtle braids, fringes, ribbons, and tassels from WENDY CUSHING, COLEFAX & FOWLER, G.P. & J. BAKER, LIBERTY, and BEAUMONT & FLETCHER.

181

ROPES, BRAIDS AND FRINGES

Ropes and cords are used for edging pelmets, finishing off fabric-covered walls and trimming cushions. Some ropes and cords have flanges, so they can be sewn in like piping on upholstered pieces.

Fan edges and short cut, or tassel fringes are also used on pelmets, both the simple and the grander swag and tail variety. They are also used on the lead edges and base of curtains – edging along the bottom of a curtain looks pretty but is not very practical – and on scatter cushions and blinds.

Braids and gimps look good placed on the edge of curtains and pelmets, and they can be stuck or sewn down to make interesting patterns on stiff pelmets. Gimps are open-work braids, either straight-edged or scrolled, and are most commonly used for finishing off upholstery.

Heavy-weight fringes, such as bullion, look particularly good around the base of sofas, armchairs and table cloths. They are usually sewn on top of the fabric skirt to give added fullness. They can look wonderful on deep pelmets and swags and tails, as long as the weights of fringe and fabric are similar and the proportions are correct.

TIEBACKS AND ROSETTES

Rosettes and other accessories such as single tassels, teamed up with a matching cord, add a stylish trim to pelmets. Use them to emphasise centre points and ends. Rope tiebacks are generally sold just as looped cords, or with a single or double matching tassel. They are normally made to tie in with fringes and cords in the same range, so co-ordination should be simple. Tiebacks should not be too tight, or the fabric will crease unattractively, and they should be set at a height that is right for the window. They usually sit better if two hooks are used per pair.

RIGHT *These bright, bold trimmings are the ones to use with colourful, floral chintzes and printed linens. Two-colour fringes will double the impact of dramatic stripes and checks, and heavy-weight multi-coloured ropes and tassels would make sumptuous tiebacks for heavy velvet or damask curtains.*

A selection of cheerful braids, ribbons, fringes and tassels from WENDY CUSHING, COLEFAX & FOWLER, G.P. & J. BAKER, LIBERTY, and BEAUMONT & FLETCHER.

GLOSSARY

ACANTHUS
Classical ornament based on the curling design of the scalloped leaves of the acanthus plant. A design frequently found in French and Italian damasks.

ACRYLIC
Synthetic fibre made from a by-product of petroleum. Often used with other fibres such as wool and cotton.

ALENÇON LACE
Fine French 17th-century lace, with a characteristic raised pattern on a tight looped net ground.

ANILINE
Synthetic dye developed in 1826 and based on coal tar. It increased the range of colours available to fabric printers and dyers, introducing variations in colour such as magenta and French purple.

APPLIQUÉ
A technique whereby patterns are formed by stitching one piece of fabric to another.

ARRAS
A town in north-eastern France (formerly known as Flanders). It was an important tapestry weaving centre in the 14th and 15th centuries.

ART NOUVEAU
A decorative style introduced in France in the 1880s, reaching its height in 1900, and remaining in vogue until World War I. It is characterised by natural curving lines, flower and leaf motifs, flowing figures and asymmetrical designs.

ARTS AND CRAFTS
A movement led and inspired by the English designer William Morris and the critic John Ruskin in the late 19th century. It was an attempt to revive skills and improve standards in the decorative arts.

BAIZE
A thick, commonly green woollen cloth with a napped or brushed finish. Mainly used for covering tables and soundproofing doors.

BARGELLO WORK
A type of needlework used mainly for upholstery, resulting in a pattern similar to flame stitch. Originally worked in silk or wool on a canvas base and common in Italy and Hungary.

BATIK
An Indonesian resist-dyeing technique using melted wax to cover areas not to be dyed. The characteristic craquelure, where the dye seeps through deliberate cracks in the wax, forms the background to bold and exotic designs. Used for clothing as well as furnishings.

BEADWORK
A form of embroidery incorporating coloured glass beads. It was popular in the 19th century for small items such as cushions, boxes, bags and mirror frames.

BERLIN WOOLWORK
A type of needlework using brightly-coloured wools and a canvas backing fabric. It was popular from the mid- to late-19th century and practised mainly by amateurs. It is so called because the coloured printed paper patterns originally came from Berlin.

BROADCLOTH
A double width, plain woollen cloth woven on a broad loom and fulled before finishing, making it very dense. Primarily produced in the west of England.

BROCADE
An elaborately patterned fabric, which is often jacquard-woven, with additional wefts that create a raised design on the background.

BROCATELLE
A lampas weave with two warps in heavier yarn creating a raised design.

BULLION
A thick twisted fringe, made from wool, cotton or synthetic fibres, used for trimming all types of soft furnishings.

CALICO
A plain weave cotton fabric, usually bleached, originating from Calcutta in India. It has been used as a base for printed fabrics since the 17th century. Today the term is more commonly used to describe cheap, plain cotton.

CHANTILLY LACE
Bobbin lace made in Chantilly, a town north of Paris, which was particularly well-known for its fine black silk lace used in Spain for mantillas.

CHENILLE
Fabric made from yarn which has a looped or cut pile, giving an effect that is soft and velvety.

CHINTZ
Taken from the Hindu word *chint*, meaning printed cloth. Now used to describe a glazed printed cotton, often with a traditional floral design.

CRETONNE
A ribbed, plain weave fabric originally made from hemp and linen, and later cotton.

CREWEL WORK
Outline embroidery in wool or cotton on a plain linen background. It was first popular in the 17th century and used exclusively for bed curtains.

DAMASK
A rich silk, wool or linen reversible fabric of two colours, in which patterns are defined by the contrast of the weft and the satin-faced warp. The name comes from the city of Damascus, where these fabrics originated.

DIMITY
A fine cotton fabric, usually white, with a corded effect created from the double or triple yarns from which it is woven.

DOBBY
A term used to describe some small patterned weaves, achieved by using a 'dobby' – an attachment to the loom that alters the lie of the warp threads.

DRALON
The trade name of an acrylic fibre used on its own or mixed with other fibres, often as a pile fabric. It is extremely durable and is popular for upholstery.

FESTOON BLIND
A swagged blind that remains swagged when let down.

FESTOON CURTAIN (Austrian blind)
A swagged blind with drawstrings that hangs flat when down.

FLANNEL
A loosely-woven woollen fabric with a nap. Associated more with clothing than furnishings.

FLAX
A herbaceous plant. One of the oldest known sources of vegetable fibre, used to make linen.

FULLING
Making cloth heavier and more compact, by shrinking, beating or pressing it during manufacture.

FUSTIAN
A coarse fabric with a linen warp and cotton weft.

GAUFFRAGE (goffering)
An embossed surface finish, achieved by compressing fabric between patterned rollers, often used on velvets.

GIMP
A narrow, openwork braid or trim used on upholstery or as an outline for lace motifs.

GINGHAM
A plain weave cotton fabric, woven with dyed yarns into checks and stripes, that originated in India.

GLAZE
A smooth lustrous finish. Once produced by polishing with rollers, it is now made by applying chemicals.

GROSGRAIN
A thick, strong ribbed fabric of silk, or silk and mohair, sometimes with a watered finish. Used for upholstery and ribbon trims.

HEMP
A plant with coarse fibres used to make rope and cloth.

HORSEHAIR (Hair canvas)
A coarse, strong fabric originally woven from long mane and tail hairs. It was incredibly durable and often used for upholstery. Nowadays the effect has been recreated using synthetic fibres.

JACQUARD
A name given to a variety of woven, patterned fabrics made on a loom using a punch card system. Invented by Joseph-Marie Jacquard in 1802.

JUTE
A strong fibrous material used to make sacking and backing for carpets.

LAMBREQUIN
A stiff, shaped pelmet that frames a window on three sides.

LAMÉ
The name given to any fabric containing metal yarns, usually gold or silver.

LAMPAS
A compound weave, generally in silk, in which wefts and warps add colour and design to the fabric.

LINEN
A strong and absorbent fabric produced from flax and used for many household textiles.

MADRAS
A plain weave cotton fabric, often brightly coloured or in checks and stripes, originating from India.

MOHAIR
A fabric woven from the hair of the angora goat, often mixed with worsted or silk yarn to produce a fluffy texture. Used for both furnishing and clothing.

MOIRÉ
A slightly ribbed fabric of silk or acetate silk mix, with a watered appearance produced by pressing the fabric through engraved rollers.

MOQUETTE
A woven pile fabric of coarse wool and linen fibres suitable for upholstery and carpeting. The pile is sometimes cut at different heights in geometric patterns.

MORDANT
A substance added during the dyeing process in order to make dyes fast.

MUSLIN
A plain weave cotton fabric with a variety of textures from coarse to very fine.

NYLON
An umbrella name for a variety of strong, lightweight synthetic fibres made from polyamide resins.

OTTOMAN
A heavy, stiff ribbed fabric with a silk warp and a cotton weft suitable for furnishing fabrics and clothing. Also the term used for a low, upholstered stool.

PAISLEY
An overall pattern based on Indian motifs in rich warm colours. Often used for shawls and throws made from fine worsted wools.

PASSEMENTERIE
The French term for braids and trimmings.

PELMET (Valance)
A piece of stiff, shaped or draped fabric placed above a door or window to hide the top of a curtain or blind. Pelmets can also be carved in wood or stamped from metal.

PERCALE
A lightweight, fine woven cotton fabric, used for bedlinen.

PILE
The fabric is woven with cut or uncut loops. There may be variations in the height of the pile forming the pattern.

PINTADO
The Portuguese word for 'spotted'; describes printed Indian cottons (chintzes).

PIQUÉ
A strong cotton or rayon fabric that has a raised geometric surface pattern.

PLAIN WEAVE
The most common of all weaves, in which the weft yarn is simply woven under and over each warp yarn.

PLUSH (Velour)
A fabric with a raised pile, similar to velvet, made from cotton, silk, wool or synthetic fibre.

POLYESTER
Synthetic fibres which are strong and crease resistant.

PONGEE
A type of woven textured silk originating from China. Very lightweight in nature, it is often used as a lining fabric or for pleated lampshades.

QUILTING
Two layers of fabric joined together with ornamental stitching and often interlined for warmth and extra bulk.

REPP
A strong fabric with a fine warp and thick weft, resulting in a pronounced rib pattern. Woven from cotton, wool or synthetic fibres, and suitable for upholstery.

ROSETTE
A decorative accessory made from offcuts of fabric used to trim and enhance pelmets and other soft furnishings.

RUCHE
A gathered strip of fabric used to trim or border curtains, cushions and upholstered pieces.

SATIN
A plain weave fabric with a cotton warp and silk or wool weft. It originated in China but was also made in Europe from the 16th century onwards. It can also be woven into a pattern, such as in damask.

SERGE
Originally a mixture of wool and worsted, suitable for men's suiting and also for upholstery.

SCOTCHGUARD
A trade name for a process that makes fabric spill- and stain-resistant. It can be sprayed onto new fabrics to give a protective layer.

SHANTUNG
A coarse silk fabric originating from China.

SILK
A strong, shiny, elastic fabric produced from yarn reeled from the cocoons of silk worms.

TAFFETA
A plain weave fabric, usually silk, with a subtle sheen and crispness. Often used for clothing.

TASSEL
A decorative accessory made from cord and fringing.

TICKING
A linen or cotton twill, usually with a fine stripe. The fabric is so densely woven that feathers and fillings cannot poke through. It is commonly used for covering bed mattresses, bolsters, pillows and other household items.

TOILE DE JOUY
A printed cotton fabric manufactured by Oberkampf at the French factory at Jouy near Versailles from 1760. It now describes monotone printed fabric with repeat patterns of romantic rustic scenes.

TWEED
A plain or twill weave woollen fabric originating in Scotland. Used mainly for clothing, but now popular for furnishings.

TWILL
A basic weave with a diagonal grain, produced by passing the weft over and under several warps in a variety of permutations.

UNION
A fabric made from mixed fibres, usually cotton and linen.

VALANCE (Dust ruffle)
A decorative fabric skirt used to conceal the base of a bed.

VELVET
A dense, rich fabric produced by a pile warp which is raised in loops during weaving by the introduction of rods. Cut velvet has loops which have been cut. Plain velvet has uncut loops which may be of differing heights.

VISCOSE
A man-made cellulose fabric which is made from wood pulp or cotton waste.

WARP
Threads which are spaced and set lengthwise on a loom forming the structural basis for the warp threads to run across.

WATERED
A wavy, lustrous finish applied by pressing the surface of a fabric with engraved rollers.

WEFT
Threads running from side to side on a loom, generally carrying the pattern.

WORSTED
A woollen cloth made from long strands of fleece that have been carded and combed. The resulting fabric is both strong and smooth.

ILLUSTRATION CREDITS

All photographs have been taken specially for this book by Andreas von Einsiedel, except for the following which appear by kind permission:

Peter Aprahamian 20, 79, 82/83, 140; Arcaid, photos Richard Bryant: Mount Vernon Ladies Association of the Union 22 (top), Homewood House, Baltimore 25, Victoria House, Portland 28 and 180; The Bridgeman Art Library, The Metropolitan Museum of Art 10/11, The British Library 12 (bottom), 27 (bottom), 30 (top), 114; Chris Challis 100/101; Christie's Images 145; Michael Freeman 33; Angelo Hornak 18, 74, 118, 157; The Interior Archive, photos Fritz von der Schulenburg/Lauriston Castle 11, Fritz von der Schulenburg 16, Christopher Simon Sykes 21 (bottom), Fritz von der Schulenburg 22 (bottom), Fritz von der Shulenburg 23, Fritz von der Schulenburg 24 (both), Fritz von der Schulenburg 27 (top), Fritz von Schulenburg / designer David Mlinaric 62/63, Fritz von der Schulenburg 65, Christopher Simon Sykes 66/67, Fritz von Schulenberg / designer David Milinaric, Fritz von der Schulenburg / designer Christophe Gollut 93,

Christopher Simon Sykes 94, Fritz von der Schulenburg / designer Victoria Waymouth 103, Fritz von der Schulenburg / designer Melanie Paine 104, Fritz von der Schulenburg / designer Pru Lane-Fox 105, Ari Ashley 107, Tim Clinch 108, Fritz von der Schulenburg / designer John Stefanidis 111, Fritz von der Schulenburg 115, Fritz von der Schulenburg 124, Christopher Simon Sykes 128, Fritz von der Schulenburg 133, Fritz von der Schulenburg / designer George Cooper 151, Fritz von der Schulenburg 179; Jen Jones Antiques, Llanbydder 124 (both), 125; Andrew Lawson / Barnsley House 109; S. & O. Mathews 106; Simon McBride 7, 78, 125; Musee d'Art et d'Histoire, Geneva 14 (bottom); Nobilis-Fontan, London 172; The National Trust 12 (top), 13 (both), 14 (top), 15, 16 (top), 17, 19 (both), 28 (top), 29, 30 (bottom), 119, 129, 167; Nelson-Atkins Museum of Art, Kansas City, Missouri (purchase: Nelson Trust) 21 (top); Hugh Palmer / Le Manoir aux Quat' Saisons 110; Ianthe Ruthven 8/9, 26, 31, 32 (both), 75 (both), 84, 99, 102, 113, 132, 139, 140 141, 156; Elizabeth Whiting Associates 150, 158, 164, 166.

ACKNOWLEDGEMENTS

My thanks go to everyone at Collins & Brown who have helped in creating this book, in particular Cindy Richards, the Editorial Director, for doing such a wonderful job in co-ordinating the 'team' and Christine Wood the designer.

I would also like to thank my editor Alexandra Parsons who does a wonderful job in gently nagging me to produce the text, Andreas von Einsiedel whose excellent photography adds an enormous sense of richness of style to the book, and Philippa Lewis for her careful selection of pictures.

My thanks also go to both clients and friends for kindly allowing us to photograph their houses and to Jacky Boase for her assistance in styling.

Lastly, I would like to express my gratitude to the Antique Textile Company and to HRW Antiques for the loan of the cushions and chair shown on the front jacket, and to all the fabric companies listed below for kindly lending samples for the fabric section.

Anna French, Anta, Beaumont & Fletcher, Bennison, Brochier, J. Brooke Fairbairn & Co., Brunswig & Fils, Celia Birtwell, Chanée Ducrocq, Colefax & Fowler, Coromandel, Design Archives, L. Dubelli, Firifiss, Fired Earth, G. P. & J. Baker, G. S. W. Co. Ltd, Home Collection/Collezione Antiques, Ian Mankin, The Isle Mill, JAB, Jean Monro, Jim Thompson, John Stefanidis, Lelievre, Liberty, Malabar, Manuel Canovas, Marvic, Monkwell, Mrs Monroe, Mulberry, Nina Campbell, Nobilis, Osborne & Little, J. Pansu, Parkertex Fabrics, Percheron, Pierre Frey, Ralph Lauren, R F Romo, Sahco Hesslein, Sanderson, Shirley Liger, The Silk Gallery, Simon Playle, Titley & Marr, Tryed Textiles, Warner Fabrics, Wendy Cushing, Zimmer & Rohde and Zoffany.

If any further information is needed about any of the fabrics listed then please contact Woodstock Designs at: 7 High Street, Woodstock, Oxfordshire OX20 1TE or Grey Watkins Ltd, D&D Building, 979 3rd Avenue, NY, NY 10022.

The author and the publishers would like to thank the following people for kindly allowing their homes to be photographed: Mr and Mrs Nicholas Jones, Mr and Mrs Christopher Shale, Mr and Mrs John Steel, Mrs Marianne Hodgson, Mr and Mrs Antonio Floirendo, Mr and Mrs Carlo Ceresa, Mr and Mrs Mavrolean.

INDEX

Major references are in **bold print**.

Adam, Robert 19, 23
American fashions
    18th C. 18, 22, 23, 120, 122-3
    19th C. 24-5, 26, 28, 30, 132
    20th C. 33, 94, 156, 178
Amish quilts 122-3
Anta designs 154-5
Arras tapestry 114
Art Deco 132
Art Nouveau 30, 32-3
Arts and Crafts Movement 30-2, 114,
    120, 166
Associated Artists company 30

Baker, G.P. & J., designs 120-1, 142-3,
    148-9, 160-1, 164-5, 172-3, 174-5,
    180-1, 182-3
bathrooms **100-5**, 125
Bayeux Tapestry 13
Beale, Margaret 118-19
Beaumont & Fletcher designs 134-5,
    146-7, 152-3, 154-5, 162-3, 168-9,
    180-1, 182-3
Beauvais tapestries 18, 114
bedrooms **80-99**, 125, 156-7, 158, 166-7
    early bedchambers 14-15, 20-1
beds
    history 14-15, 16, 22
    four-poster 14-15, 80-1, 84-5, 90-1,
        118
bed curtains (hangings)
    history 12, 13, 14, 21, 22-3, 27, 33,
        118, 166
    materials 80-1, 84-5, 86-7, 91, 92-3,
        94, 126, 138-9, 158, 166
bed linen 12, 13, 80, 82, 94-5
bedspreads 80, 86-7, 90-1, 93, 98-9,
    125, 148
    quilted 91, 96, **122-4**, 164
Bennison designs 168
Berlin woolwork 118-20
Bing, Samuel 32-3
Birtwell, Celia, designs 126-7
Blair Castle, Scotland 118
Blenheim Palace 18
blinds 22, 74-5, 100-1, 102-3,
    104-5, 142
Boucher, François 19, 114
boutis 122
braids *see* trimmings
brocade **132-7**, 138, 144

Brochier designs 140-1
Brooke Fairbairn & Co. designs 136-7
Brunswig & Fils designs 126-7
Burne-Jones, Sir Edward 30, 114

calico 59
Campbell, Nina, designs 126-7
Canovas, Manuel, designs 146-7, 148-9,
    162-3, 176-7
canvas 78-9, 106, 118, 166
carpets and rugs
    early French carpets 18
    bedrooms 84-5, 87, 92-3
    dining rooms 66-7, 72-3
    garden 110-11
    halls and studies 62-3, 76-7
    living rooms 36-7, 40-1, 46-7, 59,
        150, 154
Cartwright, Lili 27
Castle Coole, N. Ireland 75
Castle Ward, Ireland 28-9
ceiling, tented 79
chairs
    coverings
        chintz 36-7, 40-1, 74-5, 160, 162
        cotton 54, 56-7, 59, 78-9, 110-11,
        160, 172
        damask and brocade 134, 136
        linen 36-7, 54-5, 168
        moiré 38-9
        tapestry 13, 47, 116
        tartan 66-7, 154
        tweed 152
        velvet 42-3, 76-7, 128, 130
        weaves 146
    garden 106, 108-9, 110-11
    history 14-16, 21, 22, 26, 28
    in rooms
        bedrooms 82-3
        dining rooms 66-7, 70
        halls 76-7
        kitchens 74-5
        living rooms 36-7, 40-1, 47
Chanée Ducrocq designs 130-1, 134-5,
    136-7, 146-7, 176-7
checks 38, 59, 61, 70, 75, **172-3**
chenille 28-9, **128-30**, 150, *see also*
    velvet
chintz 33, 54, **156-65**, 182-3, *see also*
    Toile de Jouy
    chair and sofa coverings 36-7, 40-1,
        74-5, 160, 162
    curtains and bedcurtains 68-9, 74-5,
        84-5, 90-1, 96, 100

tablecloth 104
Chippendale, Thomas 21
Clausen, Sir George 30
Colefax and Fowler designs 44, 136-7,
    160-1, 162-3, 164-5, 168-9, 172-3,
    174-5, 180-1, 182-3
Coleman, Samuel 30
Coromandel designs 120-1
cotton **156-65**, *see also* calico; chenille;
    chintz; damask; muslin and voile;
    Toile de Jouy; velvet
    history 23, 28, 33, 54, 132, 138,
        156, 166
    bed covers and curtains 82-3, 85,
        86-7, 122-3, 164
    chair covers 54, 56-7, 59, 78-9,
        110-11, 160, 172
    crewel work 120
    curtains 46-7, 56-7, 62-3, 64-5, 72-3,
        75, 76-7, 86-7, 92-3, 98-9, 160
    cushion covers 54, 56-7, 65, 75, 85,
        108-9, 110-11, 162
    hammock 106-7
    lampshades 94-5
    throws 61
    wall fabric 72-3
Craftsman Workshops 30
crewel work 120
curtains, *see also* bed curtains; blinds;
    trimmings
    history and examples 14, 22, 23, 24,
        28, 31
    materials
        calico 59
        chintz 68-9, 74-5, 84-5, 90-1,
        96, 100
        cotton 46-7, 56-7, 62-3, 64-5,
        72-3, 75, 76-7, 86-7, 92-3,
        98-9, 160
        crewel work 120
        crochet 98-9
        damask 46-7, 52-3, 134, 162,
        178, 182
        lace 56-7, 78-9, 92-3, 125
        linen 44-5, 54-5, 56-7, 76-7, 168
        muslin and voile 23, 24-5, 28,
        56-7, 78-9, 92-3, 104-5,
        125-6
        silk 36-7, 40-1, 42-3, 50-1, 70,
        132-3, 138-9, 140, 142, 162
        stripes 174
        tapestry 76, 116, 178-9
        Toile de Jouy 94
        velvet 62-3, 128, 130, 182

weaves 68-9, 146, 148, 154
with poles 54-5, 88, 98-9, 116, 168
in rooms
    bathrooms 104-5
    bedrooms 84-5, 86-7, 88-9, 90-1,
        92-3, 94, 98-9, 125
    dining rooms 68-9, 70-1, 72-3, 116
    halls 76-7, 116
    kitchens 75, 76-7
    living rooms 36-7, 40-1, 42-3, 44-5,
        46-8, 50-1, 54-5, 56-7
    staircases 79
    studies 62-3, 64-5
Cushing, Wendy, designs 130-1, 136-7,
    176-7, 180-1, 182-3
cushions, see also trimmings
    history 14, 16
    scatter 40-1, 47, 51, 60-1, 76, 85, 116,
        134, 136
    seat 38-9, 62-3, 74-5, 78-9, 150
    squab 16, 108-9, 110-11, 158
cushion covers
    history 12, 13, 22
    materials
        chenille 128, 150
        cotton and chintz 54, 56-7, 65, 75,
            85, 108-9, 110-11, 162
        damask and brocade 134, 136
        linen 170
        moiré 38-9, 84-5
        tapestry 51
    rooms
        kitchens 74-5
        living rooms 38-9, 40-1, 47, 51,
            54, 60-1
    studies 62-3, 65

dacron 123
damask **132-7**, 138, 144, 150
    historical examples 14, 16, 18, 19, 21,
        22, 28, 128, 132-3
    curtains 46-7, 52-3, 134, 162, 178, 182
    sofas and chairs 46-7, 48-9, 134, 166
    wallpaper 76-7
de Forest, Lockwood 30
Design Archives 134-5, 160-1
D.G. Distribution designs 176-7
dining rooms **66-73**, 116
drapery 22, 24-5, 27, see also bed
    curtains
Durham whitework quilts 122
Dutch designs 14, 18, 26, 40-1,
    46-7, 132
dyeing methods 27, 30, 54, 152, 154, 170

Dyrham Park 14, 16-17

Eastlake, Charles 30
embroidery 114, **118-21**, 125, 132
    curtain panels 84-5
    cushion covers 61
    historical examples 12, 13, 30,
        118-19, 176

farthingale chairs 14
festoon curtain 14
Fired Earth designs 120-1, 176-7
Firifiss designs 174-5
floor coverings, see also carpets and
    rugs
    tiles 78-9
    vinyl 74-5, 100-1
Fortuny, Mariano 128
Fortuny printed cotton 72-3
Fragonard, Jean 54
French, Anna, designs 126-7
French design
    17th C. and before 12-13, 14, 16, 122,
        125, 138
    18th-20th C. 18, 24, 27, 30, 54, 134,
        156, 178
Frey, Pierre, designs 148-9, 158-9,
    170-1, 172-3, 174-5
fringing see trimmings
Froissart, Jean 13

gardens **106-12**
Genoa velvet 128
Georgian style 18, 32, 33
gimps 182
glazed cotton 156-7, see also chintz
Gobelin tapestries 18, 19, 22, 114
Gothic Revival style 26, 28-9
Great Exhibition (1851) 27
Greek Revival style 26
Gripsholm Castle, Stockholm 22
G.S.W. Co. Ltd. design 134-5

halls **76-9**, 116
Ham House: Queen's Closet 16
hammock 106-7
Hardwick Hall 12, 13, 150
Heal & Co 166
Het Loo, Holland 26
Home Collection/Collezione Antiques
    designs 134-5
Homewood House, USA 24-5
House of Monymusk, Scotland 66-7

Indian influence 120, 122, 125-6,
    156, 176
Ireland
    damask industry 132
    house designs 28-9, 75, 84-5, 86, 100
Isle Mill designs 152-3, 154-5
Italian design
    17th C. and before 13, 14, 128, 132,
        138, 144, 150
    18th-20th C. 18, 68-9, 125, 178

JAB designs 130-1, 134-5, 136-7, 140-1,
    146-7, 162-3, 174-5, 176-7
Jacquard, Joseph-Marie, and jacquard
    weave 40-1, 68-9, 144, 176
Japanese influence 33, 122

Kedleston Hall 19
kitchens **74-5**
Knole House 16, 128-9

lace 21, 28, **125-7**, see also muslin and
    voile
    curtains 56-7, 78-9, 92-3, 125
lampas 14, 144
lampshades 33, 42-3, 46-7, 85, 94-5
Lanhydrock 28
Lasalle, Philippe de 134
Lauren, Ralph, designs 152-3, 154-5,
    168-9, 174-5, 176-7
Lebrun, Charles 114
Lelievre designs 116-17
Liberty designs 116-17, 142-3, 160-1,
    164-5, 168-9, 172-3, 174-5, 180-1,
    182-3
Liger, Shirley, designs 126-7
linen 21, 128, 130, 132, **166-71**, 182-3,
    see also damask
    chair and sofa coverings 36-7, 40-1,
        54-5, 56-7, 59, 168
    curtains 44-5, 54-5, 56-7, 168
living rooms **36-61**
love seats 28

Mackintosh, Charles Rennie 32
Malabar designs 172-3, 174-5
Malmaison, France 27
Mankin, Ian, designs 172-3
Manoir aux Quat' Saisons, Le 110
Mantua silk 140
Marvic designs 120-1, 160-1
Mechlin lace 125
mirrors 72-3, 100-1
Mlinaric, David 156

mohair velvet 62-3
moiré (watered silk) 38-9, 47, 82-3, 84-5, 140, 174
Monkwell designs 148-9, 174-5
Monro, Jean, designs 158-9, 160-1
Monroe, Mrs, designs 158-9, 162-3, 164-5
Morris, William 30, 31, 114, 118-19, 120, 144, 166
Mount Vernon, USA 22
Mulberry designs 130-1, 148-9, 154-5, 160-1, 162-3, 176-7
muslin and voile 104, **125-7**, 138, *see also* lace
 curtains and blinds 23, 24-5, 28, 56-7, 78-9, 92-3, 104-5, 125-6
 quilts and bedhangings 80-1

Neo-Classicism 23
Nobilis designs 170-1
Nostell Priory 20-1
Nottingham lace 125

Oberkampf, Christophe 54
Osborne & Little designs 130-1, 146-7
Osterley Park 19
ottomans *see* sofas and ottomans

paintings 21, 27, 30, 54
paisleys 106, 144, **176-7**
Pansu, J., designs 116-17
Parkertex designs 134-5, 142-3, 172-3
passementerie see trimmings
patchwork and quilting **122-3**
pelmets 14, 24, 28, 182, *see also* swags and tails
 box 64-5
 materials
  cottons 59, 90, 104-5, 160
  silk 40-1, 43, 180-1
  other 104-5, 130, 174
 proportions 38, 43, 44-5, 96
Percheron designs 126-7, 130-1, 136-7, 140-1, 146-7, 162-3, 168-9, 170-1, 172-3
pintadoes 156
Playle, Simon, designs 126-7
plush buttoning 28
Point de Venise 125
polyester 125
printing 14, 27, 54, 156
punto in aria 125

Queen Anne' style 32
quilting and patchwork **122-4**, *see also* bedspreads

ribbed ottoman 52
Rococo style 18, 26, 33, 134
Romo, RF, designs 116-17
rope trims *see* trimmings
rosettes 43, 91, 182
Rossetti, Dante Gabriel 166
Royal School of Needlework 30, 118-19
Roycrofters 30
Rubelli, L., designs 170-1
rugs *see* carpets and rugs
Ruskin, John 30

Sahco Hesslein designs 130-1, 140-1
Sanderson designs 148-9, 170-1
satin 116, 122, 128, 140
Scotland
 'Glasgow' school 32
 house designs 66-7, 75, 118
 lacemaking and weaving 28, 132, 152, 154-5, 176
Shaker style 33
silk **138-43**, *see also* chenille; damask; moiré; satin; taffeta; tapestries
 bed covers and curtains 82-3, 84-5, 98, 122-3, 138-9
 curtains 36-7, 40-1, 42-3, 50-1, 70, 132-3, 138-9, 140, 142, 162
 early hangings 12, 13, 14, 18, 24, 26, 31, 118-19, 138
 lampshades 42-3
 trimmings 178, 180
Silk Gallery design 142-3
Skansen Museum, Stockholm 24
slub weave 140
Smith, George 138
sofas and ottomans
 early examples 19, 21, 28, 136
 bedrooms 82-3, 84-5
 living rooms 36-7, 40-1, 46-7, 48-9, 52-3, 56-7, 58-9, 61
 studies 65, 150
Standen House 118-19
Stefandis, John, designs 146-7
Stickley, Gustav 30
stools 28, 38-9, 51, 86-7
stripes 21, 23, 38, 41, 43, 47, 82-3, 86-7, **174-5**
studies and dens **62-5**, 150
swags and tails, *see also* curtains; pelmets

early swagging 24
bathroom 100, 104
bedrooms 138-9
dining rooms 68-9
living rooms 37-8, 38-9, 42-3, 46-7, 50-1, 52-3, 178, 182
studies 62-3
swatch board 41

tables 28, 46-7, 74-5, 96-7, 104, 106-7, 110-11
table cloths
 history 13, 128
 designs 43, 70, 74-5, 80-1, 94-5, 104
 materials 70, 128, 130, 132, 134, 142, 148, 162, 164, 170
taffeta 22, 50-1, 138, 140
tails *see* swags and tails
tapestries **114-16**
 chair and cushion coverings 47, 51, 116
 curtains 76, 116, 178-9
 history and examples 12-13, 14, 18, 19, 22, 66-7, 114
tartans 66-7, 98, 150, **154-5**
tassels
 bell-pulls 178
 ceiling and walls 79, 102
 curtains 22, 68-9, 178-9, 180-1, 182
 cushions and chairs 61, 128-9
 garden umbrellas 110
 tiebacks 38-9, 46-7, 48-9, 62-3
technological advances
 17th-18th C. 14, 54, 126, 138, 156
 19th-20th C. 26, 27, 30, 33, 120, 125, 156-7
Thompson, Jim, designs 140-1, 142-3
throws 37, 59, 60-1, 76-7, 84-5, 106-7, 152, 154, 176
ticking 174
tiebacks 38-9, 44-5, 46-7, 48-9, 62-3, 86-7, 92-3, 125, 138, 178, 182
Tiffany, Louis 30, 32
tiles 75, 78-9
Titley & Marr designs 146-7, 154-5
Toile de Jouy 54-5, 65, 80-1, 86-7, 94, 96-7, 156
trimmings 16, 24, 27, **178-83**
 bedspread 91
 chairs and sofas 36-7, 40-1, 47, 52, 109, 180
 checks 172
 curtains 36-7, 44-5, 51, 62-3, 68-9, 70-1, 72-3, 76, 91, 130, 178

cushions 57, 61, 108-9, 130, 136, 182
garden umbrellas 110
linen and lace 125, 126, 168
rope trims 43, 44-5, 48-9, 62-3, 65,
    82-3, 178-9, 182-3
tablecloths 42-3, 164
trompe-l'oeil ceiling 79
Troy, Jean-François de 21
Tryed Textiles designs 158-9
tweed 152-3

umbrellas, garden 106, 110
upholstery: history 14-16
Utrecht velvet 128

velvet **128-31**, *see also* chenille
    chair coverings 42-3, 56-7, 76-7,
        128-9, 130

curtains 62-3, 128, 130, 182
historical use 12, 13, 14, 16, 18, 21,
    22, 122, 128, 138
Victoria House, USA 28, 178
vinyl floor coverings 74-5, 100-1
voile *see* muslin and voile

wall coverings 72-3, 74-5, 78-9, 154, *see
    also* wallpaper
wall hangings, *see also* tapestries
    history 12, 13, 14, 22, 26, 27, 30,
        118-19, 128, 166, 170
wallpaper
    history 22, 30
    bathrooms 100-1
    bedrooms 80-1, 86-7, 92-3, 96-7
    halls 76-7
    living rooms 54-5, 62-3, 164

Warner Fabrics designs 160-1
watered silk *see* moiré
weaves, patterned 40-1, 68-9, 140, **144-8**
Webb, Philip 31
Welsh quilts 122, 123
Wheeler, Candace 30
Wightwick Manor 166-7
windows 14, 24, 46-7, 50-1, 65, 79, 160
wood
    garden furniture 106
    panelling 14, 70, 76-7, 168
wool 12-13, 18, 28, 118-20, **150-5**, 176,
    see also chenille; damask;
        tapestries; velvet

Ziegler carpet 72-3
Zimmer & Rohde designs 164-5
Zoffany designs 158-9, 172-3